IN TOUCH WITH ETERNITY
Contact with Another World

Visionary and Poet
Stephen O'Brien

G000244733

𝒱oices

PO Box 8, Swansea, SA1 1BL, UK

'IN TOUCH WITH ETERNITY'
A VOICES BOOK
ISBN: 0-9536620-2-0

PRINTING HISTORY
Bantam Books first edition published 1992
Bantam Books edition reprinted 1993 & 1994
Voices Books New Revised Edition published 2000

Typeset by *Voices*
In 10.5/11.5 pt Century Schoolbook.

Reproduced, printed and bound
in Great Britain by Cox & Wyman Ltd,
Reading, Berkshire

*To the Everlasting Love
that will not let us go...*

Acknowledgements

I wish to express my deepest thanks and gratitude to all my friends, in both worlds, whose continuing warmth and encouragement has supported me while giving the Message of the Spirit to millions of souls in need.

You'll never know how much your love strengthened and healed me through some of the difficult times in my life.

At my journey's end, when I finally return Home, if any soul claims a measure of spiritual knowledge or comfort from my work then know that I couldn't have done it without you.

What we share is something very special.

Thank you for being there when I needed you.

Stephen O'Brien
'Willowtrees'
Wales, January 2000

Contents

Truth builds her Nest
only in
the Branches of an Open Mind...
and as a Gift to those who Love her
she will set their Spirits Free

Stephen O'Brien

Prologue

Tonight at 7.30 while lively music plays, backstage I will walk through a rabbit-warren of dimly-lit corridors leading from my dressing room, up onto a short flight of stairs and out into the wings of another big theatre. And in the semi-darkness I will patiently wait behind the closed, red velvet curtains...

Tonight has now arrived – and I am standing here, backstage.

Beyond the lighted drapes, hundreds of people are seated in the buzzing crowd. Each face a stranger; each soul speaking to his neighbour, or silently waiting, hoping or praying that the man about to make his entrance will make contact with his dear ones. They are thinking about their people who have, perhaps, suffered some dreadful pain or tragedy and then passed out of this world and into some invisible place Beyond...

Backstage, in the semi-darkness, my heart is thudding against my chest, while my mind spins like radar. I'm desperately seeking the sound of voices not of this world: gentle, still small voices. I want to hear the tones of souls whom I sense standing close to me, spirit people who want me to tell their loved ones tonight that their lives didn't end when they 'died'. They want them to know that they are still conscious beings who live now in Eternity, that they still care for, and visit, their families each day.

Suddenly the music stops and the seconds quickly tick away towards the start of another evening of mediumship.

Stealthily, I position myself at the centre of the red curtains and I become aware of the loud announcement which starts to introduce me to the crowds. Having heard it so many times before, I now send out my silent prayers, which start rising through the world of the soul towards the Great Spirit.

'May I be of service to the people. May I help them to realise that Love is the Greatest Power in the Universe — a power even stronger than death.'

Beyond the curtains, the once-noisy public voices are now stilled. They're eagerly awaiting my entrance. Hope is rising in their breasts. They may have read one of my books, witnessed my work on television or radio, or seen my picture in a magazine; and now they are actually here, tonight, sitting in the meeting-place and clutching their tickets, which some of them see as passports to hope.

They are silently willing me to succeed, and their anticipation can be felt. They're happy to be here.

But I, the medium, am standing alone in the shadows with a great weight bearing down upon my mind. Away from the bright spotlights, in my everyday life, I'm in danger of losing my home because of financial difficulties; my body is tired through excessive work; my soul needs rest. My mind is stung with the news that my elderly father lies close to death on a bed of pain, far away from this theatre. But I cannot be beside him to offer any solace: I must be here, tonight, to fulfil my spiritual obligations.

Deep down, my heart is weeping; but I must hold back my emotions, keep them in check, and, somewhere from the depths of my spirit, I must dredge up a smile and place it on my face...

'God, who dwells in silence, knows I've

always tried my best. He will send me His strength. He will not let me down.'

The public don't want to know my personal troubles. And I will never show them. Tonight they're hoping that some of their own problems will be solved.

Suddenly my thoughts are broken by a loud voice over a microphone:

'Ladies and gentlemen, would you please welcome the man who hears Voices from Heaven — Mr Stephen O'Brien.'

My name has been called. Hundreds of people are applauding; and in an instant the big curtains sweep aside and flood the flower-decked stage with brilliant light and my form is picked out in a bright spotlight.

Out in the darkness some people are cheering and whistling in their seats. Seas of smiling strangers are focusing their attention upon me. Through the noise, a few who've travelled hundreds of miles are waving in the hope that I'll see them despite the powerful lights.

I do; my eyes sparkle in return, especially for them, and I incline my head.

It has begun.

I raise my hands and smile, acknowledging their welcome as I step towards the microphone. My heart is much quieter now, and from deep within me a warm expression rises to my face, responding to the warmth of the crowd.

Suddenly, my vision blurs behind a wall of gratitude as the noise gradually fades away and dies...

There is silence in the theatre.

Then, just before I speak — for a fleeting moment only — my own problems flash into my mind again, intense in their private pain.

But I, the medium, must cast these aside and smile while my heart is weeping; for now I am a servant and the public are waiting. I have donned the cloak of service to work for them, these hundreds who are eager to hear the great news that there is an *Eternal Life for All*.

The medium must rise above his own feelings, and try to mend the sorrowing hearts of those who are before him.

In the silence I take a deep breath, compose myself, and I'm ready to begin — for the public are waiting, and so are the people in the next world...

PART ONE

A Bridge Between Two Worlds

1

A Young Boy's Blue-Sky Days

The little girl with wispy blonde hair
suddenly appeared at the side of the stage,
surrounded by a silver-blue light. I was
right in the middle of delivering a spirit
message when she caught my eye. Guessing
that no one else in the theatre was aware of
her presence, I sent out a thought to this
beautiful child:

'I'll be with you in a minute,' I said. 'Make
yourself comfortable and be patient, there's
a good girl.'

She wrinkled her nose with a smile, then
flounced her ringlets and contentedly sat
down on the front of the apron, very pleased
I'd noticed her. With her legs now dangling
over the side of the stage, she leaned
forward and gazed around the theatre,
peering thoughtfully into the dim
auditorium. Even in a flash of a second I
particularly noticed the sky-blue ribbons

holding back her locks, ribbons that perfectly matched her brilliant blue eyes which twinkled with fun as they scanned the rows of people.

After I finished one spirit message from the Other Side and the audience applauded I re-established my link with this child, who was now sitting upright and pointing an eager finger out into the darkness.

'My Mum!' she said excitedly, attracting my attention. 'My Mum's out there! She's up in the gallery with Nana!'

Shading my eyes with a hand, I peered through the dazzling spotlights as best I could.

'There's someone in the balcony who's lost a little girl of about six years old,' I said. 'She's got blonde bouncy ringlets and blue bows in her hair; and she's wearing a blue gingham-check party-dress. "It's my birthday today," she says.'

Immediately, an arm started waving back and forth in the shadows – in the very area the child had indicated – and suddenly a young woman's voice called out in the crowd:

'Yes Stephen! Here I am!'

As soon as this was said the spirit girl sprang to her feet and started jumping up and down – so I knew I'd found the right person.

'You're her mother, and I'm told you have family connections with America. And Nana's up there with you, too.'

'Yes!' declared a kindly older woman sitting next to the recipient, 'I am.'

'Will you step to the microphones so that I can hear you properly?' I asked. 'Please don't be shy, come forward and have a few words with me. Your daughter's here and she's excited to see you.' So they did, Nana supporting Mum who was already so overcome in anticipation of a contact from her special 'lost' child that I could see her shivering with emotion.

'Don't be nervous,' I said gently, 'just try to relax and I'll do my best to link you all together. Your girl's getting really excited here, but I'll see what I can do...'

Fortunately the youngster had tuned into my mental wavelengths very well, making it one of those delightful occasions when I could hear spirit voices quite clearly.

'She was only six, but she says: "They've let me come to see you, Mummy, because today's my birthday. I'm seven!"'

The two women were dumbstruck and stared at me, open-mouthed. They could only manage a nod in agreement.

'The poor little mite passed over into the

spirit world with chest pains,' I continued; 'it was a congenital heart problem.'

'That's right,' said the ladies in quiet unison.

'And she remembers going over just before Christmas. "I didn't get to open my presents, Mummy," she says.'

'No she didn't... we lost her two days before...' said the tearful young mum, now gripping tightly onto her own mother's arm as she remembered her daughter's precious last moments on Earth.

'Well, she's not lost now,' I smiled, 'she's full of beans here and skipping about beside me – brimming with mischief. She's very happy; and she's sending you and Nana "all my love and kisses; and don't forget my Daddy," she says with a wink.'

By now, the two ladies were weeping with joy, but this clever child had another surprise in store for us – she had more unusual evidence to deliver, facts known only to her mother and herself; not even her Nana would be aware of them. After transmitting all of her love the child told us about a simple yet profoundly clever memory, one which would convince her grief-stricken family that she was indeed very much alive in another world beyond death:

19

'She's holding up some items for me to see,' I relayed, trying to focus my psychic vision. 'Ah! She's got a yellow toy duck with an orange beak; and over her other arm there's a pair of faded blue denim dungarees. Do you know why she's brought these?' I asked.

There was a slight pause while the whole theatre awaited an answer. Her Nana looked puzzled, but her Mum started sobbing and dabbing her eyes, able only to reply softly:

'Yes... Nobody knows... except me, but... I've just cleared out her old things; her clothes and toys... I gave them all away, but I just couldn't part with everything; so... I kept her yellow toy duck and her favourite pair of dungarees.'

For a brief moment an eerie stunned silence hung over the crowd, while a lump came into my throat – then spontaneous applause burst out through the hundreds of people, in full realisation that death's silent door had been flung wide open by an innocent child of seven.

Her mother breathed in shallow emotional gasps as I gazed out across the sea of faces shrouded in semi-darkness: here and there women wiped away tears, men sniffed quietly and hoped that their wives and girlfriends hadn't seen them; dozens of eyes were twinkling in reflected light.

And instantly, as though a bolt of lightning had struck my senses, I knew again why my work meant something special to these people. Somehow this link had touched their souls, moved some hidden part of themselves which often lies buried so deep beneath the thick layers of our work-a-day materialistic world.

Though for me this was just another one of the many hundreds of spirit messages I deliver each year, for these folk it was opening up a whole new world of thought. I'd been so accustomed to delivering spirit communications that I'd almost forgotten what a mind-shattering effect the first contact with the next world could have: that first thunderflash when the truth of another existence beyond death dramatically lights up the soul.

Through the applause ringing around the theatre, I remembered again just how much power mediumship possesses to change our lives for the better. It confers comfort, hope and knowledge on all those whom it touches, and somehow makes greater sense of the meaning and purpose of life on Earth.

After the meeting my two recipients stood at the end of a long line of patient people waiting for autographs. They were so profuse in their thanks, so genuinely grateful, clasping my hands and smiling and brimming with tears, that the young mum even embraced me.

'You'll never know how you've transformed my life tonight, Stephen,' she said, her own mother nodding in agreement and blinking back her tears. 'You see, after I lost my little girl, life for me was over. It got so bad I even contemplated suicide... but your message from my daughter's changed all that. It's restored my faith in God, and people – and in living again.'

What could I say?

Nothing.

I couldn't speak; there was a lump as big as an apple in my throat. I could feel the utter joy this woman projected; and I was especially moved because I'd recently been moaning to myself about how tired and stressful my public life was, mainly because of my mediumship, and now here I was confronted again with the very heart-rending reasons for doing it.

In just a few moments, I felt all at once humbled, re-kindled to carry on with my calling, and also thoroughly ashamed of my selfishness.

'God bless you both, and your daughter,'

was all I could manage.

But something else had stirred within me, too – something wonderful. In that dark theatre I'd been reminded of how a single communication from the next world can work a silent miracle. The true test of any spirit message is how much it changes the lives of those who receive it, for the better. Like thirsty watered flowers, the happiness of the two ladies before me had been visibly quenched: it was now blooming and growing again; and they'd also added to their store of spiritual knowledge. Beyond any shadow of doubt, their souls had been touched. They would never be the same people again; and so my job as a medium was done.

Since the 1970s, and more recently to coincide with the publication of my books, I've travelled many thousands of miles throughout Britain bringing messages like this from the next world to countless people in theatres, city halls, leisure complexes, spiritual churches and conference centres. Over the years, I've met and given messages to interesting folk from all over the world, sometimes to people who were house-hold names or media celebrities, and I've had to get used to receiving their thanks. But my answer to any praise has always been the same: 'Please thank your loved ones; *they* did all the hard work, I only delivered it.'

I'm proud of the work I do, but there's been a price to pay and there have been many setbacks, too. As a very private man, one of the biggest problems I've had to learn to cope with is being a familiar public face and voice, caused by guest appearances on networked TV and radio shows. Television is a powerful medium, bringing you right into millions of living rooms at once and making you a part of the viewer's family. This has produced a regular prolific postbag of sometimes hundreds of letters a week.

People's letters are serious, funny, cheerful, sad and revealing or deeply tragic. Sometimes they're desperately personal: you would expect correspondents to speak about their psychic and spiritual experiences, but some people have written about nervous depression, rape, psychosis and even sexual abuse in childhood.

But many contain profuse thanks for my being able to shed a little light into cruelly darkened lives; and I must confess that at the end of the day a sincere 'thank you' does mean a lot because it shows that I've done my work properly. Yet so much of this 'acclaim' belongs not to me but to the dedicated, compassionate spirit people who have relinquished their right to live in higher worlds in eternity to stay close to the Earth to help me with my calling.

Granted, as a team, we aren't always as successful as we'd like to be – not all spirit messages are as clear or detailed as the young girl's which I've just mentioned – but we always try our best; and often under some very difficult circumstances.

Appearances on the media have often proved stressful for such a private man as myself. And it's still an unnerving surprise to see my photograph in public places. After filming for one TV programme in Manchester I discovered that my train was delayed at Crewe (no surprises there from British Rail!) so I strolled into the station bookstore only to be confronted by a large portrait of myself, staring down from the wall. 'Over 50 million people have witnessed his amazing psychic powers,' said the publicity card. I was taken aback, but before I could leave the assistant called across, 'Will you sign them, please?'

'Certainly,' I said, squeezing out an embarrassed smile as I dumped three heavy bags onto the floor.

She was quite young and obviously excited to have an author in her store. 'They're best-sellers you know, Stephen. Your first book's been out for two years – re-printed four times in the first year, I hear – and it's still selling. Quite a feat in these days of recession, if I might say so,' she gushed enthusiastically. 'Seen you on the telly. By the way, you look much nicer on the box!'

We shook hands and I dashed out quickly to catch my train.

I find being recognised such an ordeal; I think I'd rather face my own 'death' than a horde of fanatical followers any day – but then, I'm not afraid to die.

I know I'll pass into another dimension where I'll glance back at my life and sigh: 'Well, whatever they say about you now, at least you tried your best to help a few souls along the way; God knows.' Up yonder, perhaps I'll wonder how many people truly understood what I tried to achieve, what everyone in the spiritual fields hopes to accomplish. Will they have realised that a sensitive's work is filled with deeper spiritual purpose and implications? Will they have known that mediums aren't seaside fortune-tellers, or will they still confuse the two?

Mediums consciously co-operate with spirit people to join two worlds together in an effort to prove the continued survival of the soul beyond death. And because of these contacts with progressed minds we're able to share their wisdom, knowledge, philosophy and way of life, which, they hope, will help to spiritualise humanity and the planet on which it lives. 'We are trying to raise man morally, spiritually, emotionally, mentally and spiritually,' says my spirit guardian angel, loyal friend and teacher, a splendid but ancient Native American Indian whose tribal name was White Owl.

After I'm gone I'll no doubt smile, as I often do now, at the way some folk expected me to be strange, weird or mysterious, when all the time I was just an ordinary man expressing the powers of the spirit. The world wrongly labels these powers as 'supernormal', but spiritual and mediumistic abilities are perfectly natural functions of the mind and soul. One day everyone will regain these talents and will see, sense and hear the people in the Beyond, just as our ancestors did in antiquity before the worship of materialism suppressed such gifts.

But all this, as yet, lies ahead of us.

I've come a long way since my birth into a Welsh family during a thunderstorm. I was brought up in a working class family.

27

Everyone on our estate barely scraped a living to survive from day to day, working very hard for every penny they earned. As I recall their struggles, other memories flicker onto the screen of my mind, too; elusive butterfly memories of my childhood days: those bright-eyed seasons when everything was sunny and carefree and nothing really mattered, even though we were poor. Everything looked so big then, and I was so small and painfully thin. But I cared nothing for worldly pressures. I was carefree, and free – as free as the sea birds that rose on hot thermal breezes high above the bays of my home town, Swansea, in South Wales.

In those endless summer days, I could run where liked, be what I liked, and do what I wanted. The whole wide world and everything in it was mine. How happy I'd be today if I could fully recapture this innocent wonder. If only I could experience again a young boy's amazement when he discovers a hidden nest of starling's eggs, or hears for the very first time the distant jangling sounds of a gypsy funfair with its pungent smells of toffee-apples and candy-floss. Or hear again the chiming music of neon-lit merry-go-rounds, the whirring of the big wheel and the noisy dodgem cars. How marvellous it would be to re-live his wide-eyed wonder as he looked up through young eyes at a brilliant sun in cloudless blue skies and, instead of it, saw a Spanish galleon in full sail crossing the heavens. It seemed to me then that problems just didn't exist, and life was good.

Even now, the taste of sticky toffee-apples lingers with me still, and I recall the pure joy of knowing that I was King of the Stars for a day. Like all young children, I felt that nobody could tell me what to do with the sky or cliffs; the entire planet was mine, as small as I was. The trees, the sky, the creatures in the fields – they belonged to me, and I belonged to them. We were all a part of one another; and if someone hurt them – they also hurt me.

Glancing back, I can visualise myself as a boy: that small-framed lad with a sometimes serious expression; unless he smiled, when his hazel-green eyes twinkled with mischief.

Full of vibrant life, his high-spirited nervous energy rushed him through his youth at whirlwind speed, or else so terribly exhausted him that he felt he couldn't move. And although he was 'a proper little chatterbox' who expressed thoughts fearlessly, at other times he was such a silent child, completely engrossed in his painting, drawing, reading or thinking. In a way, he was strangely 'lost'; and standing utterly alone.

But he loved his mother more than words could ever say; and his closest childhood companion – a docile cat named Tibby, on whom he lavished untold affection. I can still see before me his eyes wide open in surprise at the incredible miracle of birth, as Tibby's five or six shaky wet kittens stumbled blindly into a newspaper-lined cardboard box. The joy on his face at the sounds of delighted purring and licking as his faithful companion proudly washed her children's fur will remain with him for ever.

Many times this youngster dreamed in the stillness. He loved his own company; but then he'd suddenly want to run, skip and jump through the sunshine or else sit by a blazing coal fire in the humble kitchen on freezing winter nights, cuddled into the crook of his mother's arm, with Tibby purring in his lap.

Sometimes now, at sunset, in the quiet of an adult evening my mind can still feel the golden hot sands under this boy's feet, or know again his perceptive eyes as they search for sea-polished green glass thrown up onto the beach. I can sense again the glow of warm bricks in a high sea wall as he strove to climb it, just for the joy of it. Mighty in his success, I watch him stand upon the summit – his face wreathed in smiles – and with a cry of triumph, arms out-stretched to the sky, he shouts to the world: 'I made it! I did it!'

As a youngster, something wonderful was moving through his days; something so vibrantly real, yet strangely intangible – a silver thread of freedom. I followed the wind wherever she led, dancing through my green years like the flat throwing-stones which first skimmed the foaming waves, then sunk into silent graves like his innocent dreams and hopes...

A Young Boy's Blue-Sky Days

A barefoot boychild skips through yellow sands
Like a pony in the meadow,
Joylight dancing in his hands;
Greengrassed laughter sings across the bay:
'An endless summer of blue-sky days'.

Shining like a brightstar, he's piercing the haze,
Running through the sunshine
And scattering its rays;

Laughing at flatstones skimming the waves,
Dancing on waters way out far,

31

Then smuggling gold in hidden caves,
And lying on the night cliffs, counting stars...

Spreading rainbow gossamer-wings,
He's flying fast through sapling years
So careless, wild and free –
'Ere manhood brings its midnight-blue
Through a door marked 'dull-dark key'.

Yet still he dreams of preserving his Now
To breathe it again in unborn years,
Like the perfumed scent of sweet bouquets,
Filling his future with youthful pleasure
And joylight mem'ries that will ever measure
A young boy's glorious blue-sky days.

In the dusk of twilight, even now my mind sometimes projects haunting voices from the past; groups of children's voices long since gone, yet strangely still alive:

'On the mountain
Stands a lady,
Who she is we do not know,
All she wants is gold and silver
All she wants is a nice young man...'

'Stephen! John! Come on you two boys! Your dinner's been on the table for half an hour! Come in! It'll be freezing cold!'
'In a minute, Mam!'
'A minute's not quick enough! It's on the

plate for thirty seconds – then it's in the fire!'

'*Oh, Mam!*'

> 'Good King Wenceslas looked out
> On the Feast of Stephen;
> When the snow lay round about,
> Deep and crisp and even...'

'Mam! Mam, look! He's been! He's been! Look what he brought me. *Look, Mam!*' And I shook her awake at 4 a.m. to see the toy she'd secretly placed at my bedside just two hours earlier on Christmas Eve. 'Look, it's a fireman! *See!* You turn this key and he walks up the big yellow ladder by himself: *see!*'

Click, click, click:

'Look: there he goes!' and the cheap clockwork fireman obliged, jerkily lifting his legs as the key in his side jiggered and spun around.

There was a film of sleep over my mother's green eyes.

'Oh yes, son... lovely. Now go back to bed, there's a good boy... it isn't dawn yet...' And she turned over, burying her tiredness under the sheets, as my father snored and I dashed back to my bedroom to wake my only brother:

'John! *John*! Look at my fireman!'

But John, true to form, was completely unconscious...

> 'The big ship sails down the ally-ally-oo
> The ally-ally-oo,
> The ally-ally-oo.
> The big ship sails down the ally-ally-oo
> On the last day of September...'

'This boy is sick,' said the doctor's deep voice.

My mother looked anxiously across at him as he shone the bright torchlight into my dilated eyes.

'He nearly caught scarlet fever.'

Through delirium, I twisted my aching head back and forth, and just for that moment nothing mattered. Filled with a great and drowning helplessness I only remember thinking, 'If I'm going to die, please God – let it be quick.' And I flapped my weakened arm around outside the makeshift bed on the sofa until my mother grasped it lovingly in her own. Then I felt safer, as the doctor's voice snapped me back to reality.

'What have you been doing, young man?'

'I was only... playing...'

'Who with?'

'My friends...'

My mother frowned and put her hand to her mouth. 'Oh; I forgot about those.'

The doctor willed an explanation from me.

'Me and Leighton collected bluebottles... in a jar. We were going to let them go, honest we were...'

My mother looked embarrassed as the doctor said, 'That's where he got this temperature. But don't worry, Mrs O'Brien; I think he'll survive.' And then to me: 'Being kind to animals is one thing, Stephen, but you've been a silly boy; they carry germs, you know.'

Two full-mooned adults glowered down at me, faces pale, as I uttered weakly:

'But they... the animals are our friends...'

And the last thing I remember was my mother's soft kiss planting itself on my burning-hot forehead – then I fell into a deep and swimming sleep...

Isn't it odd how some memories float back, yet others remain buried away somewhere secret, never to return? Or are they completely gone and lost for ever, I wonder? Perhaps not; at least, not psychically:

In the 1970s, when I was in my twenties, I awoke one morning from a haunting 'dream' which had stirred my soul and profoundly moved me. My childhood days – and my

35

wonderfully kind mother with them – had long since vanished from the Earth, but on that strange night I found myself fully conscious inside an incredible series of visions of my youth. Somehow I'd been spiritually transported back into former years when I was a boy and she was still alive. It was an unforgettable experience that remains with me to this day, even though it occurred while I was physically sound asleep.

In my psychic 'dream', I was amazed to find myself standing in the centre of our old kitchen where I'd lived as a lad in the late 1950s. Everything around me was so vividly clear and real: the threadbare matting over the oilcloth floor, the coal fire with its smoky smell and its crackling sticks burning in the grate. Every detail, without exception, was exactly as it had been twenty years previously; even the faded wallpaper which had hung on the wall since long before my birth; and the quaint, battered brass candlesticks on the mantelpiece, next to the clock that always ticked too slow.

And there behind the small television table was the big sash-cord window which overlooked a raised concrete yard with a steep drop onto our weed-bound garden.

How enormous that window had looked when I was a child; and how small and insignificant it seemed to me now.

Through it shone a sun-kissed day with a gentle breeze outside which swayed our rickety washing-line back and forth in the back-garden. At the bottom of our garden was another garden: rows and rows of back-to-back terraced houses trailing away; old houses, badly repaired and poorly furnished – like our own – and full of working-class folk who scraped together a few shillings to feed hungry mouths. Money was tight in those days and my parents did backbreaking work for very little pay.

At the foot of the garden was our tumble-down outside toilet, just as I remembered it: a tin-sheeting and brick affair which froze you half to death in the winter when cold Christmas snows whipped in through the gaps in its battered door.

I sighed deeply as I gazed at the old place and absorbed the poignant sights and sounds of yesteryear. But on this night – as my physical body lay fast asleep – here was I *right in the middle of the moving pictures, sounds and feelings of my boyhood*; and this marvellous experience made me want to weep in gratitude for the wonderful memories strangely mine again. But I suppressed my feelings for fear of breaking this spiritual experience.

Everything before me was so tangible and real: I could breathe in the musty smells of the coal fire as it crackled in the grate, and the wafts of cooking passing through the rooms from our small scullery watered my mouth.

But these 'living' things were surely the fabric of the past and not of the present?

Then I turned and faced the dusty two-seater settee for there was a bustling sound nearby. Motionless and completely at a loss to describe my amazement, I silently watched as my dear mother fussed in from the tiny scullery. Here she was, standing before me, my own mother – but young again as she'd been in my youth. She wore a bright blue-and-white flowery-print short-sleeved 1950s dress, belted at the waist and full-skirted; and she walked across to the round mirror over the fireplace and pushed her fingers through her dark springy hair. Her clearbright eyes and high cheekbones were glowing with radiant health as she then pottered around the small kitchen, tidying things up, unable to sense or see me.

It was all so miraculous, so breathtakingly vivid: she was actually present and everything was wonderfully clear. Yet I couldn't speak; I could hardly breathe... My mother, 'Mam', was living once more, passing before me in a waking dream: moving, existing, breathing – *alive again*.

Fully conscious of every detail I felt powerful emotions rising within me almost to bursting-point; I wanted to speak with her. I wanted to say how much I'd loved her, how much I'd missed her since she'd 'died' of agonising cancer at forty-nine years old. I wanted to tell her how wonderful she'd been and what marvellous love, trust and loyalty she'd given her children. How I wished I could have moved my mouth and said: 'Mam – it's me; Steve... Mam, I love you... It's so good to see you again.'

But nothing would come; not a single word...

Just then, scuffling footsteps clattered down the long passageway leading from the green front door, past the little parlour, and into our kitchen – and a moment later a spritely young boy arrived in the sunny room, panting and wiping the sweat from his brow with a bare arm. He'd been running like fury down the street.

I was thunderstruck as I beheld the form of my own former self – me, as a boy of six years old.

Disbelievingly, I shivered as I leaned forward and searched the young lad's face: his sad green-brown eyes, his features, the shape of his head, the sloping round-shoulders covered by a loose, yellow open-necked summer shirt, and his thin bare legs lost inside wide short trousers – and I thought my heart had stopped beating. And I remember thinking, 'My God, it *is*... It's *me*...'

Fixing my gaze on the youngster's eyes and the freckles on his skin, I marvelled at his slender form. Here was a living person; he was breathing; he was present – not as a shadow but as a real little boy. Yet how could this be? My mind couldn't grasp the immensity of what was happening.

Then suddenly these thoughts were broken by my mother's familiar voice.

'Stephen, wash your hands now, there's a good boy. Your dinner's nearly ready.'

'What is it, Mam?' asked the child brightly.

'Beans-on-toast. I haven't had time to go to the shops yet.'

'*Oh great!*' And the little body dashed out into the scullery, leaned up and drew some water from the big tap and fumbled with a large bar of green soap, while my mother puckered up settee cushions with sharp dusty slaps.

My adult self, half afraid to breathe, moved cautiously across to the scullery door and peeked inside, just to gaze in wonder at the young lad stretching up on tip-toes and making a clumsy job of washing his hands over the metal sink. It *was* me: but young again – six years old and pressing my lips together, deep in concentration, and splashing water everywhere as I always did.

But how could I be living *now* as a lad when I was already an adult in my twenties? Both this 'ghost' of my younger self and of my mother had long-since vanished from the Earth. So what was happening?

Though deeply confused and lost for an answer, I consciously stopped my thoughts in their tracks then just accepted the beauty and simplicity of it all, savouring for ever the images being strangely granted to me. However they were occurring didn't matter now – I just immersed myself in them with deep gratitude, relishing every moment of the unfolding scene through misted eyes; and for the first time in many years I felt the warmth of true happiness inside.

Powerful emotions rose in my breast as

the little boy before me – totally unaware of the presence of his larger self and the big wide world awaiting him – wiped his young hands. I had an overwhelming desire to stretch out my arms and touch him. I wanted to embrace myself. I wanted to hold him close and plant a gentle kiss upon his brow and tell him about what, as yet, lay ahead of him in life's road: the grief, the joys; his writings brought about by links with minds beyond death. The media people; the press and the sceptics; and the years of national touring, declaring to millions of people the message of eternal life; and all of this counter-balanced by floods of affection from the public; and so much laughter and many tears, all waiting to be shed.

I wanted to prepare him for his future life. I longed to make him promise with all his heart that he'd always love and cherish his mother, all of his days; and that he should never say one unkind word to her (as I knew full well that he often would).

How I ached to press him to my heart as if to soothe away the troubles he was yet to know.

All these things I wanted, but I could have none of them, for my time amongst these strange images was quickly dissolving; it was spent, and – without warning – this unforgettable psychic journey was over all too soon.

The scenes quickly shifted and faded out into blackness as I lost touch with my visions, my feelings and my past.

Suddenly the kitchen and everything in it had gone.

Everything was silent; and I remembered not another thing...

*In the eyes of a Child
the Universe and All its Wonders
are Contained...*

2

A Little Child Shall Lead Them

Dreamily, in a semi-tranced state, I was standing on the windswept street, swaying gently while muffled voices floated past me. I was mentally so far away that all my thoughts centred on 'How on earth will I get through this day without collapsing of exhaustion?' I'd been on my feet since 4 a.m. and I'd already driven hundreds of miles and was now standing in the middle of a film crew briefing session at two o'clock in the afternoon on a damp and blustery street in Manchester. I was barely conscious: I'd already been working ten hours and the day wasn't half over yet.

Suddenly the director's voice broke my reverie:

'*Stephen!*'

I blinked, uncomprehendingly, stretched the tension from my neck then faced him with full attention.

'Sorry, Peter; I was in a little world of my own then.'

'As I was saying,' he resumed, 'once the camera's running, drive the car down the road, around the corner then stop outside the guest-house, ring the bell and go inside; and we'll shoot everything.'

This was how the London-based film crew started its documentary on my work; and I did as I was instructed – four times. But filming is always a long and tedious process: I was already dog-tired but I still had a meeting to take near Manchester later that day. Earlier, I'd been interviewed on radio and when we got to the guest-house the film crew were already anxiously awaiting us: me, Jeff Rees Jones, my tour manager, and another helper who was working with us on this tiring stretch of my 1991 nationwide tour.

'Now look, Stephen,' said Peter, whose director's tone smarted me back to reality again, 'we don't want to get in your way but we'll follow your every move today – so just act naturally.'

'But how can I when there's a camera running, a great big boom with a microphone stuck on the end of it swinging over our heads or wiggling under our noses and a lighting man with his assistant flitting in and out, plus yourself? It's hardly natural, is it?'

'Just forget us, and it's business as usual.'

So we did. Mind you, we kept bumping into them every five minutes or walking into shots we weren't supposed to be in and we got under their feet all day. At one point, later in the theatre before the public arrived, I'd been on-stage chatting in an interview to camera and then I left it to go and get changed, but quickly bounced back on asking: 'Was that OK then?'

'Get off! We're still filming!' they shouted. So I sneaked away...

The film was supposed to be a sort of 'Day in the Life of' documentary, introducing the kind of work I do to a wider public, showing its pressures and stresses as well as the education, comfort and joy that I try to give to people. That venue was just one meeting out of forty-five which I conducted during 1991 to coincide with the publication of my second book, *Voices from Heaven*.

The producer had said from the start: 'I'm not making a promotional film, Stephen, it's a balanced view of one of your days'; and this meant that a handful of Christian Fundamentalist picket-line protestors who were gathered outside the hall also got a chance to air their views.

But the most amusing episode was when Jeff commented on-stage, in a private chat to camera before the meeting started, that 'Stephen can be difficult to work with because he's such a perfectionist, you see.' He then proceeded to arrange pots of white flowering plants around the set while delivering a caustic aside to the camera: 'You watch now, I bet when he comes down he changes all these around!' And true to form, *I did*.

My only disappointment with recorded shows is that the television people never transmit any of the spirit messages in full, but rather in piece-meal clips. How can people hope to judge life's vital issues from an incomplete picture?

But 'live' television also has its difficulties. Over the years when I've demonstrated on programmes, sometimes the results have been good but they could never be regarded as first-class mediumship because of the difficult conditions under which they took place. When the clock's against you and 'instant' results are demanded by millions, an immense amount stress is created in a sensitive's mind, which adversely affects spirit contact.

And asking mediums to deliver immediate

results on an entertainment show is rather like asking Beethoven to compose the opening strains of a new symphony in four minutes or less. I doubt that he could do it.

I've spent more time turning down media requests than I have accepting them because television audiences seek enjoyment, not communication; and their attitudes are not as reverent as they should be when attempting to contact loved ones in another world.

Nevertheless, I suppose even one tiny ray of light is precious to those who stand in spiritual darkness and are searching.

The spirit world certainly brought light and hope to one couple in the theatre later that night, and the film crew witnessed it.

One of the most moving messages was delivered from the Other Side of Life by a little boy to both his parents, who were called forward to the microphone. I'd heard a spirit voice giving me the names of 'Taylor' and 'Jean' and assumed that my communicator may have been called 'Jean Taylor'.

Sometimes the conditions for spiritual contact aren't ideal and voices are either faint or not as clear as I'd like them to be. However, Jean told me that she'd brought 'a little boy who'd died from heart difficulties;

he passed over after some surgery'. His mum stood up and I called her forward, but before she moved I knew that the boy also wanted to speak with his Dad:

'Is his dad there? Let's have his dad, please. He's calling for him, too.' As the young couple stepped to the front of the hall, the look of hope on their expectant faces moved me. What then followed was an emotional and poignant message. I thought I heard the little boy say something that sounded like 'Adam and Eve'. Even though the phrase seemed like nonsense I've worked with the spirit people long enough to know that when they really want to communicate they'll use any means at their command. So I repeated his words, which brought an immediate response from his Mum:

'Adam was his name!' she called out.

Then the young lad told me about someone called 'Watson'.

'What does the name of Watson mean to you?' I asked.

'His first consultant's name was Mr Watson.'

I then felt happier about relaying the rest of the lad's message:

'Mr Watson did his best. Don't blame Mr Watson.'

The young parents said they didn't; and little Adam joyously called out to me:

'*I'm six!*'

His mum said he was five when he had 'died' and that his sixth birthday was approaching in just over a month's time.

'Buy him a birthday cake, Mum,' I said, 'and put six candles on it and light them because he'll be there and it'll mean the world to him to know you've not forgotten.'

By now they were tearful, but young Adam went on to describe more details, including the exact way in which his dad had held his hands as he lay in the hospital bed. I nearly added my own tears when I felt a powerful wave of love flowing out from Adam towards his parents, then back to him from them. It was such a moving contact.

Adam's parents, Karen and Aiden Taylor, were enthralled by their son's message and delighted to receive from the stage-set a large bouquet of flowers, which I presented to them after the meeting.

At the end of the meeting, while the film crew questioned a queue of people clutching books and tapes they wanted autographed, as well as other folk who were waiting for a few words and a handshake, I noticed the director filming an interview with Adam's parents. When they'd finished I joined them and instinctively gave Karen a kiss on the cheek and sympathised with Aiden; they were two such lovely people. I shook their hands and chatted about their little boy.

Karen produced two photographs of her son, one of which he'd already said during his message that he didn't like: he was pulling a face on it, not like the other one where he was smartly dressed in his football gear, holding up his dad's trophy pleased as punch. Through tears Karen unfolded his sad story and what the message had meant to them:

'We saw an advert in the *Manchester Evening News* that mentioned your book, *Voices from Heaven,* and I immediately bought it in W. H. Smith's, plus your first book, *Visions of Another World*; and we decided to come.

'This is the first time we've seen you. We'd hoped so much to get a message from our son tonight – and we got it.' Her voice faltered, and while she dried her eyes her husband spoke:

'More importantly: you see, tonight it's eleven weeks to the day that Adam died.' And his tears, too, could not be held any longer. My heart went out to the young couple.

'Never think of your boy as "dead",' I said, 'because he's not. He's still very close to you. Why don't you visit your local Spiritualist Churches and give him more opportunities to contact you again? I'm only here for one evening but now that he's managed to get through I'm sure he'll want another chance.'

A flicker of wariness moved across their eyes at my suggestion, but it soon dissolved away.

'Spiritualists are quite friendly folk, you know,' I said.

After half an hour we parted amicably, with Karen gifting to me the photograph of young Adam dressed in his football togs.

'Don't think your link with me is ended because your son's message is over,' I said; 'write and let me know how you get on.' Then I gave them two of my poems: one called 'The Greatest Power' (Love), and another about remembering a special life called 'Do Not Forget Me'.

They left much happier than when they'd arrived; and one of the stewards they'd spoken with told me they had thought of placing the flowers I'd given them on Adam's grave. But this helper had suggested, 'Why not take them home and put them in a vase next to his picture, because he'll often pop in and see you?

Much better.' And I wholeheartedly agreed.

Here are two personal letters (combined into one) which I later received from Karen Taylor about her son's message on that night.

Sceptics please note that we had never met; they were strangers in a large crowd. And even though they could not place the spirit name of 'Jean Taylor' (the communicator who'd brought their son to greet them from the Other Side) they do share the same surname, one that I'd also taken great pains to spell out, letter by letter, during the link. I think 'Jean Taylor' might well be a distant relative of theirs.

Here's Karen, young Adam's Mum, who is happy to share her story with all those who have lost a child, in the hope that they may be helped and comforted by it.

Aiden and I went to your public meeting at Oldham on 30th April. We were both in deep despair and were searching for hope and proof of Life after Death. We lost our youngest son, Adam, on 12th February 1991 after open heart surgery at Harefield Hospital, Middlesex. Adam was only five years old and we love him so much; he always was, and will be, our Special little boy. He was born with a very serious and rare heart defect and we knew that he would need high-risk surgery when he was about four or five (he had lots of chest infections and a few spells in hospital) — but as he was such a character, so determined and such a fighter, we were convinced he would get through it all right, but he didn't.

After surgery, he clung to life for twelve days following a cardiac arrest and two very serious drops in his blood pressure; and after receiving kidney dialysis and liver massage, Adam wasn't responding at all and was put on a life-support machine. He'd also had a lot of fluid in his body and the doctors were worried that this had gone to the brain. They told us that even if he ever got off the machine and could breathe again for himself, he would almost certainly be blind, deaf and very handicapped indeed.

They said the kindest thing we could do was to allow them to switch off his life-support machine.

What a terrible decision to have to make and live with; words cannot describe our horror and how we felt. The tests they performed gave us no hope of just a slight handicap – they said we would basically just have a body to feed. What were we to do?

We went along with their advice, and our son Adam died in the operating theatre, and they removed his organs (which we felt he would have wanted to have been donated to help someone else), and I think, really, we died with him.

When we saw him later, he looked so peaceful, but how terrible we felt.

We love him so much and we're a close family, but now we're just existing, caring for our two other boys. We're so unhappy and the hurt inside is too much to bear. Our life has really ended: we both feel we have lost everything, our family is torn apart in grief, never to be the same again.

Then I saw an advertisement in the *Manchester Evening News*: you were appearing in Oldham, and we were interested now in learning as much as we could about life after death, seriously, for the first time.

We got tickets, never expecting to get a message from Adam.

That evening we went to see you, you gave us hope. Thank you, Stephen, you gave us a message that provided us with proof that Adam continues to live in another place. You said 'I have a lady called Jean Taylor here and she has a little boy with her.'

You said, 'The little boy had something wrong with his chest'. My heart was beating so fast, being a very shy person I was so frightened of standing up and putting my hand up, but I was so desperate and I'd so strongly felt I had to go and see you on that evening.

I put my hand up, I couldn't let it go if it was Adam. Then you said to me, 'I'm getting "Adam and Eve".' And I said 'His name was Adam,' and you asked us to come to the front.

We were both so nervous and I felt so shocked as the message that came through was so clearly for us: I couldn't describe how I felt. My husband, Aiden, got very emotional.

About my son's illness you said that 'a valve was blocked, and there was a hole in the heart, and the lungs were involved'. All exactly correct.

You went on to further describe Adam's heart condition, and other details, all so accurate and only we knew them. Thank you so much, Stephen.

You then said Adam was saying 'Happy Birthday' to someone. It was my Dad's birthday on the 7th of May but also on that day his brother's friend had a birthday and Adam used to play with them both.

You mentioned 'white flowers', and we said that we'd got Adam a lot of red and white flowers for the funeral – but later we learned that his grandad was growing all white chrysanthemums for Adam's grave.

You also said my son mentioned to Aiden,

my husband, 'Two hands!' What Adam meant was two hands saving goals: saving shots from his dad. Adam had some junior goals set up in the garden and he would have stayed there all day if we had let him.

Plus, on Adam's gravestone we have had a special picture done of a goalkeeper making a 'save' on one side, and a footballer kicking the ball on the opposite side, all in gold guilt.

You said that his birthday was coming soon and he would be six and that he wanted us to get him a birthday cake with six candles. It was his birthday on the 14th June, we did what he asked, but what a sad day it was: no present to give, no little head to kiss. How terrible we felt on that day; so sad.

You also mentioned: 'Don't blame Watson.' This surprised me because Adam was only five months old when Mr Watson retired, but he did diagnose what was wrong with Adam when he was a few weeks old. He was Adam's first cardiologist at the Children's Hospital.

You said, quite correctly, that we both carried Adam's picture on us and that Adam didn't like the picture that his dad had.

You said we got a sudden call to go to the hospital; this was also true – we got the phonecall on the day before.

You also said, quite correctly, that I had

something wrong with my foot. I saw you lift up your right foot and touch it — and it was my right foot that I had had trouble with for weeks. Only Aiden and I knew that.

You also said there was a grandad there too, but didn't mention him again. Both my grandads were shy personalities.

After investigation, we don't know who the Jean Taylor is; but the people next to us claimed Jean Taylor. Maybe their Jean Taylor helped our Adam to make contact. Perhaps we were all together in the hall and she met Adam and offered to help him. But whoever she is, we're so grateful to her.

We have (since) been to the Spiritualist Church a few times, to the special demonstrations with a guest medium. So far, unfortunately, we have had no (further) contact. If you are ever in the Manchester area again, we will certainly come to see you. You are such a good medium. I get the *Psychic News* now to see if you are on tour anywhere near us. I have received a lot of comfort from your books and tapes.

As you will recall at the end of the evening we gave you a picture of our Adam in his football kit, holding his Dad's trophy. Also the cameramen interviewed us; they were very nice. Do you know if the programme will be shown? I hope so, we want to tape our message to keep for ever and show his elder brother, when we think he will understand. A programme showing your mediumship, which is so outstanding, can only help other people like us in grief.

Thank you, Stephen. Please write back. Every day I go over that evening. You don't know how much you helped us that night.

I don't suppose we will ever have personal contact with a medium as good as you, unfortunately, but we thank you from the bottom of our hearts for the comfort we have received by getting the proof that our son lives on.

> Yours sincerely,
> God Bless and Take Care,
> Karen Taylor.

Placing aside my obvious embarrassment at some of Karen's remarks, I think it's important to say that if I've been able to help anyone who has 'lost' a precious loved-one I could not have done this without the compassionate support of my spirit friends.

Adam's link, of course, was very poignant, but not all spirit messages are so serious: in fact there have been countless amusing ones because people don't change immediately when they 'die'; their character and sense of humour stays with them, thank God.

I've found that positive, cheerful attitudes

and laughter in an audience actually lifts the psychic vibrations and helps good communication to take place. Laughter is a burst of high-frequency energy which gives the Other Side a power-boost and makes it easier for them to transmit clear, detailed evidence.

One night, when conditions for contact in a meeting were particularly good owing to the audience having built-up the necessary psychic power by reacting favourably to witty communicators, I was able to receive specific facts for a woman in the crowd:

'Elizabeth Johnson from the Other Side sends her greetings.'

'*I'm* Mrs Johnson, and Elizabeth is my daughter, though she's still alive on Earth.'

'But she's named after Elizabeth Johnson in the spirit world,' I said.

'No.'

'Oh, but I heard it so clearly. And she says she's watching over her name's sake – your daughter. I can tell you that this Elizabeth died in 1902.'

Just as my recipient was about to open her mouth to refuse again, her eager husband – two rows back – leaned forward, took the microphone and announced:

'That's perfectly correct, Stephen. I've been researching our family tree and

61

Elizabeth Johnson was born in 1848 and died in 1902, just as you said.'

There was spontaneous applause; a common occurrence when the spirit people are able to get such clear messages as this through to us.

But detailed evidence can also be delivered wrapped in folds of love and powerful emotion, too, as in the case of a lad of thirteen who reminded his sister of his unusual passing:

'He was just a youngster,' I said, 'and he was hit in the neck by something hard... something like glass – no wait a minute, it wasn't glass, it was a snowball. Does Robert mean anything?'

'That's him!' the astonished girl replied. 'He's my brother, and that's how he died.'

'He was catching his breath; he says, "I choked on my food".'

'Yes, he did.'

At this point, loud sobbing came from the lady next to her. 'That's my Mum,' said Robert; and indeed she was. The microphone was passed to her but she was too overcome to speak, so his sister continued answering.

Robert went on to mention 'John', and 'standing on the touch-line watching the lads playing football and having a marvellous time, and shouting them on to win!'

'John was his football-team coach,' she smiled.

'And Mum, Robert says you've had his football jersey in your hands this week. Have you?'

'Yes,' she whispered, barely recovering from the joy that her 'dead' son's message was bringing. 'I've been cleaning out his room this week... and sorting through his things.'

'Well he knew because he's been close to you all and he's telling me to say: "Please will you give my football jersey to John, Mum? I like him such a lot."'

Sympathetic sighs murmured through the crowd when his final phrases touched us all.

'I'm fine, Mum... Please don't worry about me: I love you; I love you... I love you...'

Such messages are so terribly moving, and when they're delivered you can usually hear a pin drop in the auditorium. But the mood and style can change quite quickly when a new communicator's personality is felt. Each link is different and Robert's contact was immediately followed by a humorous, whimsical granny on the Other Side who brought forward some delightfully comical memories for her special friend. I began with:

'There's a lady here with me who says she was "a char – I worked for Mr Pilkington, and he didn't pay much either!"' When I described her and relayed that she'd 'met up with Mrs Stevenson and we've had a good chat about old Pilkington,' a woman in the back of the stalls quickly responded.

'Yes, I know her. She worked for the Pilkingtons: they were wealthy landowners and Mrs Stevenson was her friend – she lived a few doors up.'

Our bubbly char then delivered more surprising statements:

'He was a (bloody) difficult man,' she announced, 'and very mean too! (I didn't say 'bloody' in public, or repeat some of her other choice language!) And I remember the time,' she went on, 'when he left some money on the sideboard to tempt me! He wanted to see if I'd pinch it! (Bloody cheek!)'

'That's quite correct,' said my recipient, 'I remember her telling me.'

'That *really* hurt me,' said granny, 'so I got my own back on him. I wanted to leave the (bloody) job but I needed his reference, see – so one day, I told him a story about his daughter that he wouldn't forget!'

'That's right,' said the smiling woman.

'And it worked a treat! He fired me *and* I

got my reference.'

There were gasps from some of the audience because she was such a good communicator, who finished up making us laugh with: 'Pilkington's over here with me now and I've given him what for and told him *exactly* what I thought of his (bloody) job, where he could (bloody) stick it and my pittance of a wage!'

Hundreds in the crowd had a good belly-laugh at her comments, probably because they'd like to have done the same thing to some of their own employers!

And of course, I laughed with them; I have an excellent sense of humour. (Even so, the other day I turned down a TV appearance which required the host to hit me over the head with a sugar-glass bottle while he joked to the audience: 'You may be clairvoyant, Stephen, but I bet you didn't see *that* coming!')

It's a good job that not all of my spirit messages are transmitted in such a light and irreverent vein; and neither are they all given in public. Some have been received privately when I'm by myself or sometimes in small circles of psychic friends who sit especially to contact the next world.

Over the years I've been given numerous messages by spirit people from all walks of life. These have included quite memorable words transmitted by some well-known figures in our world. Whenever I get a link from such people, I'm always reticent to publish; unless, of course, they ask me to do so. Dr Martin Luther King was such a communicator.

This remarkable man led a Civil Rights Movement for black people from the mid-1950s up until his death on 4th April 1968, when he was shot by an assassin in Memphis, Tennessee. Dr King didn't seem bitter about his passing, a quality that seems to link admirably with the Nobel Prize for Peace, which he was awarded in 1964. Martin maintained, preached and propounded the noble doctrine of non-violent protest to gain relief from the cruelty of racialism.

He was, and still is, a very great man; and it seems his fight to free people from oppression is continuing from his new world, as he reveals in his contact, the words of which are an inspiration to peace-loving souls everywhere:

Dr Martin Luther King:

I was only a young man when the call came for me to leave and go to the Promised Land.

Those who should have been helping me, hurled me into in the next world; but I'd seen over the mountaintops and I knew where I was going.

Through the great love I have for my own people, and all other races, creeds and colours, I tried my very best to show a way of brotherhood, a way of peaceful cohabitation between all kinds of people in all different kinds of social and racial structures.

Looking back upon those hard and difficult years – difficult for me and my dearly loved family, especially my children – I think I can say a measure of success was ours.

But the battle is not yet over.

There is more work yet to be done.

My brothers and sisters in other lands, as well as in America, are crying out '*Freedom!*'

They're calling out for '*Justice!*'

They want the bonds and shackles of oppression to be cut away from them so that they can breathe the pure air of freedom of expression.

So I shall not cease from my fight.

I have never, no not for one moment, given up my goal: that of freeing my people, and any others bonded by slavery of one form or another.

The world is a beautiful place.

The souls of men and women are beautiful.

If we can encourage this great beauty forward then all the ugliness will be purged away, as the sunlight bleaches the scorching lands of Africa.

I pray for peace and love, one towards another.

I have not rested; I shall not rest. No: I shall inspire and send my strength to everyone still engaged in the great march forward, toward the lights of freedom, truth, peace and love.

Within your Soul
Resides all the Energy of Creation,
just waiting to be Discovered . . .

3

Soul Powers

Peace, Love, Truth and Freedom are just some of the many qualities that belong to our spiritual nature. If we become aware of the inner worlds of the spirit, our own power of psychic sensitivity can build up to such a degree that we may often 'feel' or 'sense' these intangible attributes in other people.

I'm often aware of psychic impressions that reach me from this world, and not from the next – such as the time when private information was revealed to my soul-perception: I didn't know it was a secret, and I certainly didn't mean to embarrass anyone. My natural soul powers were working quite freely one day when I was introduced to a friend's young boss.

'This is my manager,' she said; and as we shook hands, I immediately became aware of his illness: it was an instantaneous thought, an inner knowing. But I didn't mention what I'd registered, not until the following Sunday when I confided in my friend:

'By the way, did you know your boss has something wrong with his chest?'

She nearly dropped her teacup.

'Yes, I do actually,' she said. Interest flickered in her eyes. 'Go on, Stephen: tell me more,' and she leaned forward in her chair.

'Well, I'm afraid he's got a heart murmur: a small hole in the heart.'

She was astounded.

'You're absolutely right. But he never speaks about it, he's only ever told one person: me. Who told you?'

'No one. When I shook his hand I immediately "knew". Perhaps it's been worrying him, or he's been thinking about it recently.'

'But *how* did you know?'

'My soul registered it.'

'Stephen, you're uncanny,' she said, and she lifted her eyes to the heavens.

Her boss, like every other life-form, is surrounded by swirling energy-fields of electro-magnetic and spiritual activity – auric fields – and some of my energies mingled with his, instantly conveying his problem to my mind.

Reading the aura is a skilful art, a useful soul-ability that takes years of careful practice to perfect. One of the easiest fields to sense is the physical aura, which contains a complete 'picture', or matrix, of a person's health problems and true character.

When we develop our psychic sensitivity we can become more aware of subtle, fine vibrations of energy that are radiated by people living in *this* world and not necessarily in the next. Auric awareness can convey an immediate and often stunningly correct 'picture' of someone's personality. All living things, and even seemingly 'dead' objects, carry their life-stories around with them. These psychic impressions are 'alive' in the mind and in the electro-magnetic fields, and once you're sensitive you can register them – and that's that; it becomes as automatic as breathing.

I vividly recall one television appearance when a wealthy man, whom I can only describe as a professional 'sceptic', offered me £250,000 to submit myself to be 'scientifically tested' by him, and I refused. How naive he was not to realise that I could see right through the open secret in his heart. As far as I was concerned he might as well have been transparent; the true motivation behind his facade was revealed clearly to me. Why didn't he speak the truth?

'Let me publicly ridicule you by twisting your results and explaining away any shred of evidence that you offer. Submit yourself to me and make me famous.'

Regrettably, a number of media people have tried to embarrass me or denigrate my work before millions of viewers. On the same TV show in the early 1990s our celebrity host sprang what was supposed to be a rather unpleasant surprise on me, announcing that there was now to be an unscheduled 'live' nationwide phone-vote on my abilities.

And the question she asked the viewing public was quite specific:

'Can Stephen O'Brien contact the spirit world? Yes, or No?'

But I don't think the producers got the result they wanted because the station's switchboards jammed with callers and they received over 8,000 votes in under twenty minutes – *about seven calls a second* – the majority of which were in my favour.

To the surprise of the sceptical producers

the public overwhelmingly supported my
work, and voted:

Yes: 82% — No: 18%

My definition of what a sceptic *should* be is:
an open-minded person who thoroughly
investigates *all* of the available evidence
then meticulously sifts it and seriously
follows through every lead until all avenues
of research are exhausted – and only then
should any conclusions be made.

I have no objection to any intelligent
person making an enquiry, provided that he
respects the truth and is also willing to
publish it, even if it's at variance with his
own opinions.

However, the popular anti-paranormalists
and 'psychic debunkers' who seem to be
proliferate on the media are simply out to
ridicule. It seems to me that they work from
the following premise: the paranormal does
not exist, therefore all evidence of its reality
must be faked.

Instead of honest investigation they prefer
to brand all sensitives and healers as liars,
cheats and charlatans; very loudly, too –
and particularly if they're getting paid for
it.

Experience has taught me that as far as
many of these professors, psychologists,

debunkers and theologians are concerned, passing examinations hasn't necessarily conferred wisdom upon them, nor common sense, or even common decency.

And I think it should be remembered that others who have modelled themselves on Harry Houdini (the prolific psychic debunker of the twentieth-century), are usually professional 'magicians' or 'escapologists' of sorts; or, to put it another way – paid deceivers and illusionists.

Perhaps we should remember that when we view their 'evidence'.

There are some academics, however, who are more fair minded. After we'd done a heated television 'debate' together, Professor Arthur Ellison, a past President of the Society for Psychical Research, leaned across and sighed over the studio applause: 'It's so sad, Stephen. All they want is entertainment, not serious discussion at all. Isn't it a load of old tosh?'

I think he has a point.

My reply one radio interviewer's comments best sums up my own feelings about the professional sceptics and psychic debunkers. With brow-knitted intensity and between probing and sometimes facile questions, my renowned host said of these people:

'Stephen – about all those hard-headed realists listening to you out there: they're highly sceptical of your powers and have no belief whatsoever in the paranormal, an afterlife, or your teachings and revelations. Now tell us – what do you think of them?'

'Poor souls,' I replied.

Untold millions of people have experienced the basic psychic ability of extra-sensory perception (ESP) or natural soul-sensing (with the obvious exception of our cynical friends). It's quite a common occurrence: you may meet a perfect stranger for the first time and though, at first, he might seem to be a happy-go-lucky character, 'something' which you sense about him makes you feel uneasy – and he later proves to be an unpleasant person.

All mediums are naturally sensitive, but in varying degrees. They can't help it; it's part and parcel of their psychic awareness. But they're not alone in possessing these abilities. I've often watched folk on street corners shaking hands: 'Oh, how lovely to see you,' they smile. But as the person turns away they pull an horrendous face at what they'd *really* felt when the contact was made.

Millions of women have this ESP,

sometimes labelling it 'feminine intuition', and my mother was no exception. I don't know about yours but mine could spot a lie at thirty paces! And there's plenty of evidence, too, indicating that psychic power frequently runs in families. My mother certainly passed hers on to me: I can recall numerous occasions when this sixth sense functioned quite spontaneously, often to my benefit, and sometimes to the amusement of others.

In the late 1980s, just after I'd passed my driving test with flying colours, I went alone on a really fast journey to 'test my wings' so to speak. But zooming along the motorway I had the sudden sensation that someone was sitting in the back of the car; I'd heard the rustling of long silk taffeta skirts. It was such a *real* sound that I pulled over onto the hard shoulder, switched off the engine, turned around and had a proper look – but there was nobody there.

Unconvinced, because those Edwardian skirts had whispered so clearly, I got out of the car, marched round to the back and opened it to check if anything was loose.

But everything was secure.

When I later told some friends, they just laughed. 'Well, you're bound to have ghostly company, aren't you? We who value our lives dearly have been praying like mad for you since the day you got behind that wheel!'

I must admit I did see the funny side of it; unlike in this next memory when my soul-powers came to the fore:

While working on the east coast of Britain, my charming hosts, Arthur and Gladys, whisked me off for a quick trip around the local beauty spots. I was delighted. We stopped near the sea and Arthur and I got out of the car to catch the ozone in our throats.

'Just follow me, Stephen, there's a smashing scenic view from up there,' he said, as we neared the dangerous cliff edge. I tentatively crept forward, craning my neck as I heard him ask, 'Well, what do you think?'

Arthur grabbed my arm while I peered down over the grass onto the distant sands some 300 feet below. Suddenly I lost sight of the drop and got an overwhelming urge to throw myself from the clifftop. Arthur quickly pulled me away from danger.

'What is it?' he asked.

'I'm all right,' I muttered, clutching the nearby shrubbery. 'But I just felt sick, as though I could have thrown myself over the cliff. I expect there are plenty of people who'd like me to do that,' I volunteered.

'Well, Stephen,' he said, 'I brought you here because this place is called Beachy Head; and that spot is known as Suicide Point. Dozens of people have jumped to their deaths from there onto the beach below.' I just looked at him.

'Let's get back to Gladys in the car,' I said, 'I need a sit down...'

These soul-powers have brought me many fascinating experiences. I remember registering another startling Place-Memory: it happened at about 3 o'clock in the morning when three friends were entertaining me (I'll stay up chatting into the early hours). We were just making a last ditch attempt to keep our eyes open without matchsticks when everyone felt incredibly relaxed.

'Something's up,' said the eldest.

'Yes, I think we should sit for the spirit people, don't you?' I suggested.

It was agreed, and after several minutes of peace and quietness – qualities which are conducive to spiritual contact – my soul powers started working and I witnessed a remarkable scene unfold before my psychic vision: it was an ancient Place-Memory.

A small band of sad bedraggled peasants, wearing ragged and dirty clothes, appeared in the energy-fields within the living room. The silent group walked across the floor, diagonally from left to right. The phantoms were moving through the space in front of me and leaving it through the wall behind me. The ten men were shouldering muddy pick-axes and shovels and they were dressed in thin soiled shirts and breeches, but they were all bare-foot. The remaining few women wore long dark skirts trailing in the thick mud and their faded black shawls were tightly wrapped around their thin shoulders to combat icy winds.

It was all so real.

In the centre of the procession some men were carrying a rough-hewn wooden coffin, quite small, and I sensed that it contained the emaciated body of a teenage girl who'd probably died of a fever.

In silence I watched the vision, too afraid to breathe lest I disturbed it. Experience told me that I hadn't 'slipped time' and been transported into a previous century, for these people were not aware of my presence; they couldn't see or sense me. No, this was a ghostly psychic picture of the past: a moving image recorded in the very atmosphere around us, projected upwards by the ground on which this modern house was standing: it was obviously built on the site of an old dirt-track road which had existed many centuries ago. Gazing at the bent and weary travellers, I knew they were heading for a burial place, which I sensed was quite nearby.

A moment later, the vision faded and I described it to the others.

'There must have been an ancient burial ground in these parts,' I said, 'in that direction,' and I pointed behind me to where the ghostly figures had dissolved through the wall.

'That's right, Stephen,' said the eldest, who was in her sixties. 'There *was* such a place many years ago; just over there, where the people were going.'

I wasn't surprised, of course, for soul powers can register all kinds of things, such as premonitions. While visiting another group of friends one Sunday morning, dreadful psychic feelings pervaded my soul.

'Whatever's the matter?' my hostess asked.

'Something awful's going to happen,' I said.

'To my family?'

'Oh no; nothing like that, though it's really bad news, like a war.'

But what I couldn't describe at the time were the emotions I felt; soul sensations are difficult to express, but I'll try. I felt as though a ferocious whirlwind had torn through my spirit and that nothing could stop it. Then there came a sense of desperate, anguished cries of the spirit, as though thousands of souls had voicelessly screamed out into the void, pleading for mercy...

This unusual premonition remained a mystery, however, until a few days later when the six o'clock news announced that the President of Iraq, Saddam Hussein, had invaded the small country of Kuwait.

'That's it...' I half-whispered, 'that's the start of destruction and carnage,' which regrettably turned out to be correct. To this day, no one knows how many souls lost their lives in the short War between Iraq and practically every other peace-loving country in the world in 1991. Millions deplored President Hussein's actions; and Iraq's state-controlled propaganda machine couldn't be trusted to release accurate figures of casualties.

But I'll never forget those horrifying television pictures of deadly American Missiles in air-strike attacks, filmed as they were fired, and screened as they blew up targets 'live'. It was too sickening for words: people were dying inside buildings as reporters proudly proclaimed, 'Yes! That's another direct hit! We sure are winning!'

Some of the laser-guided missiles were so accurate they could be seen smashing through specifically-targeted doors and windows, 'taking out' the interiors – and the people inside – but leaving the shell to stand; a wicked reminder of how little man's soul has progressed towards kindness and compassion.

The use of Allied bombs and air-strikes to force Iraq out of Kuwait continued unabated, night and day. This action was fully backed by the United Nations until the Allied Forces announced a time limit for Iraq to finally withdraw its troops from Kuwait, prior to launching a ground assault to take it back by force, in compliance with a UN Resolution. Just before the limit expired at 5 p.m. Greenwich Mean Time on Saturday, 23rd February 1991, I got a call from a New York journalist from *Harper's and Queen* magazine:

'What's going to happen, Stephen? The world is anxious and waiting,' she said.

'I fear he won't comply with the United Nation's Resolution 660 (requiring Iraq's full and unconditional withdrawal). My soul was so disturbed by my premonition and all those soundless voices crying out in anguish that I'm afraid the ground attack will start...' And, regrettably, I was right: it commenced and proceeded to claim many more innocent lives before the conflict ceased.

I've always maintained that the future casts its shadow before it, and that a sensitive mind can register it.

The spirit people, of course, can also use these same soul-energies to accomplish some other remarkable feats, like in this next case. I'd been filming for a television programme and had popped into another guest's hotel room for a chat. Tina Laurent and her husband were Electronic Voice Phenomena enthusiasts and they'd recorded many mysterious disembodied voices on audio cassettes over the years. I was oblivious to the fact that the Other Side were then drawing on my psychic powers, but Tina explained the next morning:

'I hope you don't mind, Stephen, but yesterday I secretly recorded our talk because I've often wanted to conduct an experiment with the power of a good medium. Anyway, nothing unusual happened until you closed the door on the way out –'

'And?'

' – a clear woman's spirit voice said on the

85

tape: "Oh, he's gone now."'

Though thoroughly intrigued, I simply had to smile back:

'You obviously missed part of her message.'

'What do you mean?'

'Well, she'd probably said, "*Thank God* he's gone now!"' And we had a good laugh.

It's a blessing that my spirit friends have an excellent sense of humour. Of course, they can also be quite clever, too – especially when there's a developed medium present, because sensitives shed an abundance of extra psychic light and energy around them, which can help people on the Other Side to accomplish all kinds of unexpected feats, such as the moving of physical objects supernormally. In the early 1980s when I was unemployed, hungry and my stomach rumbled like a hollow mineshaft, I had empty pockets to match my hopes. But I was surprised when a spirit voice said 'Move towards the kitchen sink'. After I obeyed, it then said 'Open the old tumble-drier'. So I did.

To my great amazement, there – right in the bottom of it, staring me in the face – was a crisp, brand-spanking-new £10 note. I laughed and threw it into the air and shouted out: 'You can do *that* again, anytime you like!' But they never did. It was merely some temporary relief to get me through a rough patch. They'd brought about this phenomena by drawing upon my soul power, which enabled them to transport the money from one place and materialise it in my home. I've no idea where they got the £10 note but it had probably been lost, and hopefully not stolen.

Although it takes a good deal of psychic energy to materialise such a spirit gift (known as an apport) can you imagine how much more power would be needed to physically levitate me? I'll never forget the night it happened.

I was fast asleep but was rudely woken about 1 a.m. by a strange awareness of several pairs of hands near my legs, arms and head. I instantly 'knew' I was about to be lifted up – so I called out indignantly: '*No:* I'm not a balloon!'

Suddenly everything went quiet again, so I turned over and drifted back to sleep, wondering what on earth the spirit people were up to. (They'd never bothered me much during the night – it was one of our understandings: bed was for sleep.) But about half an hour later we had a repeat performance, only this time much stronger.

'Don't you dare!' I called out, sitting bolt

upright. 'What are you playing at?'

Silence...

Then I fell asleep again.

The third time, I was woken up at 3 a.m. to find myself feeling as light as a feather and actually *floating* in the air. I'd been physically lifted from the bed, horizontally, as stiff as a board, and then they started sailing me off towards the door, bedclothes and all. I immediately knew they were going to dump me unceremoniously onto the bedroom floor – but I stopped it with a mighty shout.

And suddenly I bounced back down onto the mattress, puzzled but quite relieved.

I guessed there was some kind of urgent message hidden in this odd experience; the people on Other Side were trying to tell me something. It was then that I remembered I hadn't seen my father for a while, and that I really ought to pay him a visit between tour-dates. I began wondering how he was coping with his failing health... and then, somehow, I linked this unusual 'happening' with *him*, and my feelings were soon proved correct.

I'd been supernormally levitated *three* times in a row – and *three* days later my father was found close to death and was rushed into intensive care at the hospital.

Dad almost 'died': his temperature was phenomenally high but the doctors treated his chest infection just in the nick of time and saved his life.

So the riddle was solved: it had been a spiritual warning, and an unusual way of demonstrating the power of the invisible world.

This kind of psychic power, which certain mediums possess, can also be projected from the body to move physical objects, even unconsciously, *without* any spirit intervention. This often happens in what's sometimes wrongly assumed to be 'poltergeist' activity. I've investigated a number of cases and right in the centre of the action there's usually someone (frequently a teenager) in the clutches of emotional turmoil, often in the throes of puberty when major hormonal disturbances occur in the body. Troubled emotions can create and project strong soul-energies, which can then physically move objects in the house.

I know this happens because I've experienced it. Once, while standing near some large curtained windows on a sunny afternoon, I was feeling quite annoyed with someone who'd deliberately spread lies about me. I felt my trust had been betrayed – and that's when it happened.

All at once the long heavy drapes began swaying back and forth, as though a sudden breeze were passing through the room – but there were no windows or doors open and it was a perfectly calm, airless summer's day.

I stood perplexed, watching the weighty curtains billowing away of their own accord. I wondered if the spirit people were responsible, but then I realised that *my own anger was generating these forces*.

When I made conscious efforts to calm down, the drapes fell deathly still, like silent curtains in a Chapel of Rest.

Such fascinating psychic powers, because of their unusual nature, sometimes evoke unwanted reactions from people, particularly the 'medium-worshippers'. All good sensitives discourage adoration, but the compliments keep flying, I'm afraid.

I was once astounded by a middle-aged woman who, after gazing rapturously up into my face, glassy-eyed throughout one of my meetings, clasped my arm tightly at the end of the night and announced with stunning conviction: 'You are my Jesus,' – and the next instant she ran off through the crowd.

I was shaken to the core, especially as I've always taught that mediums are just ordinary people. But I guess some folk will never learn.

What the public generally don't know is that whenever these powerful psychic abilities are used, sensitives burn up their vital nervous energies, which must be carefully replaced by natural means: rest, pure water, and wholesome nutritious food.

Here's some wisdom about psychic power and a medium's health from one of my spirit friends: my guardian spirit and mentor, White Owl.

At all times seek moderation in all things. Balance is the key word. Too much work and not enough rest stresses the mind and disturbs the spirit, leaving you unfit for use by higher intelligences. Evolved spirit guides never dominate their mediums on Earth; it has to be a willing co-operation, a fine blending of minds working towards enlightening humankind.

Mediums – our priceless treasures – are carefully watched and educated to seek and maintain health, for of what use is an instrument whose personal power batteries are weak and drained? None whatsoever – which is why we counsel you to balance workloads.

Never tire yourself to the point of physical and nervous exhaustion; always be sensible.

Rest the body, relax the mind, and make sure that periods of activity are properly counterbalanced by periods of rest.

Far too many sensitives overwork their abilities, and their power resources drop below the necessary levels needed by us to make reliable attunement possible.

Quality work is produced by quality instruments, and the instrument – in order to be of good quality – must be physically, emotionally and spiritually healthy.

Tranquil mental equilibrium is of the greatest aid to us when trying to contact you.

Contact comes through the power of soul-attraction, which touches everyone whether they are sensitive or not. Every one of us is influenced to certain degrees by people from the next world: nurses and doctors in busy hospitals naturally attract the help of spirit healers; lawyers draw keen discarnate minds to inspire fights for justice. And the reverse principle is also true: dark-minded, selfish, ignorant souls draw their own kind through the Universal Law of *Like Attracts Like*.

Each of us has a general soul-vibration or, to simplify it, an average frequency of existence created by the sum of our general thoughts and feelings. Souls approximating to this frequency are naturally in attunement with us, no matter which world they live in.

In my early twenties my public work attracted a famous spirit helper from the Other Side: arguably one of Spiritualism's brilliant mediums of the twentieth-century, Estelle Roberts. She was one of the few mediums to stun Members of Parliament with some remarkably accurate survival evidence, which was largely responsible for Spiritualism becoming a state-recognised religion in Britain in 1951. Up until then public mediums could be, and sometimes were, arrested by the police under the archaic Witchcraft and Vagrancy Acts, which I'll be speaking of in a later chapter.

During her fifty years of service to the spirit world, Estelle Roberts appeared before countless thousands of people; notably at the Royal Albert Hall in London where, on a score of occasions, she filled it to capacity and people were sometimes turned away.

Since those days, a number of dedicated mediums, who were working in small Spiritualist churches to intimate groups of believers, thought they could follow in Estelle's footsteps and take the giant step to addressing such large audiences in public halls – but they did not succeed.

It is not an action I would recommend lightly. A great deal of skill and psychic development is required to accomplish this satisfactorily. Sympathetic Spiritualists are open-minded, patient and willing to test evidence with their intellect – even if the medium's information seems incorrect – but in public halls audience attitudes are quite different. As one wise veteran medium stated: 'They want precision, Stephen, and if they don't get it they'll get up and walk out.'

Estelle Roberts drew close to me from the spirit world through the *Universal Law of Attraction* because she fully understood the demands this kind of public work can place on a sensitive; and she knew I needed help.

I think it's true to say that both she and I had wisely served our apprenticeship *before* we started demonstrating survival to thousands of people.

We also share another link: we've both worked at the London headquarters of the Spiritualist Association of Great Britain, the largest association of its kind in the world. The SAGB, at 33 Belgrave Square, certainly puts sensitives through their paces, not to mention giving them an education. Though I made several guest appearances there, I was often amazed by the number of sitters who didn't have a clue about what a medium's proper function was; and this is where I used my soul-powers, as I'll explain.

Sitters come from all over the world, many wanting a psychic reading: a soul-to-soul link from psychic to sitter where the sensitive acts more or less as a 'mirror', telepathically reading facts and details from the sitters' minds and auras and then relaying them during the appointment. This doesn't involve any contact with discarnate people and has nothing to do with spirit communication. Psychics can use their own soul-powers to 'read' others (or even the vibrational fields of inanimate objects, which retain facts about their psychic history: a process called Psychometry), but mediums communicate with discarnate people. There's a world of difference and I wish more people were aware of it.

But soul-powers can prove most helpful in difficult consultations, like this one at the Association:

One bright morning my sitter was already ten minutes late when suddenly he burst in through the door, red-faced from running, threw himself into a chair and promptly arranged his overflowing Harrods carrier bags around his feet. He was a tall blond American, about twenty-five, who was out of breath as he rattled out quickly:

'Oh, I'm so *glad* to get into your schedule. I've come right across London and I was afraid I wouldn't see someone today; the traffic was dreadful!' And without a pause he continued: 'Now, what I *really* want to know is this: will I get the money to move to a New York apartment, and will I find the cash for my cosmetic surgery; plus, will I happy there and when does it happen?'

I took a breath for us both.

For the first time he was motionless, glaring hopefully across into my eyes. I couldn't believe what I'd just heard (and was thoroughly intrigued about the cosmetic surgery: he was six feet tall, blue-eyed, classically-featured with a perfectly-formed V-shaped torso and looked as though he'd just stepped out of catalogue. I wondered what pieces of himself he wanted altered. My soul powers, however, indicated he was hoping to undergo an operation to change his sex).

I eventually broke the pregnant pause.

'I don't think I can answer those questions today,' I said.

'Why not?'

'Because I don't do psychic readings here,

only mediumship.'

'Oh? Well, the lady I normally visit tells me everything I want to know.'

I maintained a diplomatic silence.

'So what about my plastic surgery, my flat and my happiness?' he asked, counting out his wishes on his fingers.

I sensed a small spiritual lesson would be in order.

'If we examine those questions,' I gently explained, 'the common link between them all is "I". Making those decisions is your own responsibility, not mine or that of the spirit people. We're personally responsible for what we think, say and do.'

After the shock had sunk in we spent the next twenty minutes discussing this concept with true American intensity; and at the end of the day he got more real spiritual help for his life than he'd bargained for when he dashed into his appointment. And when all's said and done, that's what it's all about – helping each other.

So many people mistakenly believe that mediums can solve all of their problems, but they can't. No one has all the answers, not even our loved ones on the Other Side.

Often women write: 'I'm desperate for a message from my husband. Send me his pet-name, or our children's names to prove he's alive.' But if more people understood the difficulties of communication between two worlds there wouldn't be so many unreasonable demands. It's not always easy for communicators to reach us, which is why a patient search – amongst those whose sensitivity and soul-powers have stood the test of intelligent investigation – should be made.

Many start their searches by witnessing the work of respected mediums within the Spiritualist movement.

Follow those whose work has spiritual depth and truth stamped upon it.

Seek and you will find; knock and the door will be opened – but only when the time is right.

All seekers will need plenty of patience and a realisation that nobody living in this world, or in the next, can demand instant spiritual answers.

But the solutions *will* come, because there's no barrier so vast that it can prevent us finding the ones we dearly love.

They are not lost to us: their souls are still alive. They have survived death; and we will find them again, provided we are prepared to make a thorough and intelligent investigation.

I Will Wait For You

I will wait for you...
   Though we never had a chance to say goodbye,
Remember me...

When winter snows are falling through a quiet sky
I'll remember you
   when, in our darkest hour,
   you held my hand and prayed I wouldn't go –
      but a silent voice called out to me
      that my time had come,
      and I had to travel Home...

Since then,
I know your life has never been the same,
for I visit you each day:
      so many times I've felt your pain;
      I've watched you cry;
      and I've heard you call my name...

But now, further along life's road I stand
in a timeless world, just beyond your sight,
      waiting for the day when I can take your hand
      and bring you across
      to this Land of the Golden Light...

Till then, remember me, you understand –
and try not to cry.
      But if you do:
      Let your tears fall
      For the happiness and the joy that we knew,
      And for the special Love we shared –
         For Love can never die.

The Spirit Within You
is the Spirit of the Breeze,
the Soul of the Sky;
in Essence,
We are All the Same...

4

Talking Animals

Animals have souls, too; and they possess soul-powers. They're spirits working through physical bodies just like us; and, like us, they also survive death. They have a conscious awareness of themselves, akin to that of man.

In my first book, *Visions of Another World*, I devoted a whole chapter to stories of their spirit-returns to their beloved human friends, recording incidents of pit ponies and even elephants and giraffes successfully communicating.

To those who think that animals have no intellect, let me say: you are wrong. In Sylvia Barbanell's excellent little book *When your Animal Dies* (Psychic Press Ltd) she introduces fascinating animals who could actually talk through a system of paw-tapping and, in the case of dogs, barking out loud to indicate letters of the alphabet and hence they spelled out words. Take the story of a little dog called Lola, for example, whose remarkable gifts are well worth recalling.

Extracts appear from Henny Kindermann's book *The Story of Lola*, translated into English by Agnes Blake, in which Lola's bright intelligence astounds us with answers to profound questions such as:

'Lola, would you like to be a human being?'
'No.'
'Why not?'
'Because of work.'
'Lola, do you belong to me?'
'No.' (energetically)
'To whom do you belong then?'
'To myself.'

Further stunning replies were gained when the little dog was questioned about the vital issues of life, death, and the existence of the soul:

'Lola, what will become of you when you are dead? What will become of your body?'
'I will go to heaven.'
'Do you know what a soul is?'
'Yes.'
'Have I a soul?'
'Yes.'
'Has a stone one?'
'No.'

'And a horse?'

'Yes.'

'And water?'

'No.'

'Have all dogs?'

'Yes.'

But Lola's clever intellect and caring heart were most startlingly revealed when probably one of the most important powers in the universe was touched upon. Her answer profoundly shames beyond words all those who are cruel to animals.

'Lola, what do dogs feel when they look at the eyes and see the sorrows of people?'

'We feel Love...'

These amazing replies are clearly interwoven with intelligence and feeling, powerful forces which spring from an active thinking mind. But there are no surprises here to sensitives who have often read the trusting thoughts of our fellow brethren, the animals. Ask anyone who lives close to the land and they'll tell you of the bright keen minds which their animals possess; animals like Kurwenal of Weimar, a clever and humorous little dachshund who belonged to Mathilde, the Baroness von Freytag-Loringhoven. She taught Kurwenal to speak in a language of barks which corresponded to the letters of the alphabet; and he expressed many surprising opinions. Several eminent minds questioned him, including a scientist who asked the little dog:

'What do you think about a dog's soul?'

'It is eternal, like the soul of man.'

And when the Baroness probed his opinions concerning deeper religious matters, Kurwenal astonished her by replying:

'I often pray.'

'What do you pray for?' she asked.

'... For you,' said her beloved friend.

But such loyalty and love were not the only feelings expressed in thoughts by Kurwenal. By all accounts, the little dachshund displayed a great and active interest in all human conversations, and on more than one occasion he revealed his ability to fully understand speech. During one discussion, Professor Max Müller – a veterinary surgeon – stopped to ask the dog for his views on a rather morbid subject: the guests had been speaking about dogs being eaten as delicacies in some Eastern countries. Said the Professor to Kurwenal:

'Do you wish to say something about it?'

'Yes,' he replied, then stunningly said, 'the Christian religion prohibits killing.'

An incredible and mind-boggling response,

I think you'll agree.

They say that the dog has long been regarded as man's best friend, and maybe they're right. Certainly Mr Wisniewski from Poland had a remarkably loving and loyal companion; a mongrel dog called Burek who would never leave his master's side. Wherever one went, the other was sure to follow, ambling behind; they were an inseparable pair, like father and son. But sadly, after a short illness, Mr Wisniewski died, and for a fortnight his faithful dog went missing. Friends and neighbours hunted high and low, searching the countryside for Burek but they couldn't find him anywhere.

Worried because he might be freezing, hungry, cold and grieving, someone was inspired to set off in another direction... and there in the cemetery, lying across his master's grave, poor Burek was found close to death. Emaciated and on the point of collapse, he refused to leave his master's side. 'Come on, boy,' they said gently, 'your master's gone away, and won't be coming back now...' — and only then did the loyal Burek allow himself to be tenderly lifted and carried home to be fed, washed and cared for.

Who could ever forget such wonderful love

and devotion?

In a strange kind of way perhaps Burek's great reward was forthcoming, for the next day the old dog 'died' peacefully and went to join his beloved friend and companion in the Beyond.

What a remarkable creature. But perhaps no more so than an ordinary chatty budgerigar named Twink (!) who shared her life with a Mrs Passmore. Twink was loved by everyone because of her endearing characteristics, especially when she did her popular and clever party-piece which usually proved to be quite a show-stopper! When requested (politely) she'd recite the entire *Lord's Prayer*, often at such great speed that sometimes she would stumble over a difficult phrase and call for some human prompting. Then she'd carry on right to the very last sentence and would even remember to say 'Amen'.

Twink also recognised humans whenever they approached, suddenly exclaiming things like 'The rentman's coming!' (when he was); or 'Georgie's here!' (when Mrs Passmore's son paid an unexpected visit).

Such wonderful examples of our brethren's bright and happy ways make it so hurtful to contemplate the cruelty dealt by uncaring man to dear little souls like Twink,

Kurwenal and Lola. But I'm afraid we humans are a long way from giving our friends the kindness and respect they truly deserve, as was clearly highlighted to me by someone recently.

'It happened in a busy Hong Kong market-place and it disgusted me beyond words,' she said.

'A British soldier and his eight-year-old son were walking past the stalls when the little boy spied a small puppy and instantly fell in love with its big sad eyes. He pleaded with his dad, "Please, Daddy, can I have the little dog? Can I have him?"

'Eventually his dad gave in and the boy smiled into one of the cages, pointing out his puppy to the stall-holder who – in a trice – grabbed it by the scruff of its neck, squealing, then threw it onto a wooden board and chopped off its head in front of the horrified child.'

My heart skipped a beat. I couldn't believe what I was hearing.

'And as if this wasn't barbaric enough, he then took a sharp machete and skinned the puppy. The shocked boy was inconsolable, racked with heart-rending tears and his father was so stunned that he simply led him away.'

I was equally appalled, loving animals as I

do. How could the soldier justify this cruel act to his sensitive son without admitting man's wicked disregard for Animal Rights? He could not. No one with the slightest degree of sensitivity could. There's no excuse for such cruelty yet it continues all over the world each and every day.

Another similar degrading incident reached my ears recently. It caused a woman I know to be physically sick in a Bangkok market-place where she watched a man as he ordered some of the crudely advertised 'Hot Crispy Snacks for Sale'. Filling the order, the merchant scooped up a handful of day-old chirping, naked baby chicks and automatically tossed them alive into a wok full of burning oil.

I make no apologies for recording these hateful acts so graphically. The only way to make people sit up, take notice and then do something to stop these travesties is to present the shocking facts. Hopefully, soul-revulsion may birth a new saviour for our brethren; perhaps caring people will either form or join pressure groups, canvass and sign petitions as well as write to these barbaric governments and do everything possible to stop the mass murder of the innocents.

Some insensitive people still declare that

animals operate with instinct alone. What absolute nonsense this is: they have individual minds and personalities. When Mr Bryson died (he founded the animal sanctuary where my wilful but loveable cat, Sooty, came from) many helpless creatures he'd saved from degradation, death and slaughter paid their last respects to him on his funeral journey. They owed him the greatest debt of all, the gift of their lives, and they wouldn't let it go unheeded because they knew he was their friend. (Once, he'd travelled from England to France just to rescue one old horse from being slaughtered.)

A pall of sadness fell over the sanctuary on the day of his final procession. The many animals he'd helped became quiet: Percy the pig (on whose back children used to ride) was silent; so were the ponies, a goat, and the huge cattery as well as all the dogs. And as Mr Bryson's cortege moved along streets lined with grateful people and their beloved pets, the hearse went past some fields when something wonderful happened. Horses and ponies, whose lives he'd saved, trotted to the edge of the fencing and stood silently watching, as if to say 'Goodbye' to the man who'd shown them so much love and kindness.

What greater tribute could any man wish?

Somewhere in a book it's written that God marks even the smallest sparrow's fall, something else that I accept because I've had evidence of it. Once when driving fast down the motorway late on a cloudy moonless night, all at once a spirit voice urgently told me to 'Swerve to the right!' My body instantly reacted – just in time to see the moon break cover and pick out three starlings grouped in close formation zooming past my windscreen within inches of sudden death. If I hadn't obeyed that voice, I'd have killed them outright.

How much more then will God, I wonder, through His ministering angels in Spirit care for us, His children, when such tender concern is shown for our animal brethren?

It's through the exercise of our compassion that we forge closer relationships with all life-forms, but how I wish more of us were as kind to animals as my medium friend Clare is. She actually took the trouble to set a wild rat's broken leg in a splint (made from two matchsticks and some sellotape) then fed and nursed it until its limb healed. She later released the creature back onto the waste-ground where it had been found in obvious distress a month earlier.

Can you imagine how grateful that tiny

animal must have been to her human friend after receiving such tender loving care? If only everyone was this kind to our brethren they'd spiritually evolve much faster; they would advance in leaps and bounds – and so would we.

There's a great deal we can all do to help the animal kingdom with its spiritual progression – each one of us can do something positive, starting today, if we really care about these souls.

I well remember a discussion I had with a meat-eater a few years back: it took place a few days before Christmas near a busy shopping mall. Delicate snowflakes spiralled through the bitterly cold streets which were thronged with last-minute shoppers breathing steam as they walked by.

The woman had just bought a huge oven-ready turkey for her family's Christmas dinner and the dead bird was so big that it filled her shopping bag.

We began discussing spirituality and she asked me if I had any ideas that would help her to progress in this way. When I spoke about kindness to animals, she refused to accept that these creatures had souls, even though mankind has been presented with masses of convincing evidence of their survival.

'I just can't see,' she said, 'how on earth *my* spiritual progression could be connected to being kind to animals.'

I was happy to enlighten her.

'Spiritually developed souls would not create the commercial demands which force others to kill and torture sentient creatures for profit,' I said.

'But what part do I play in all of this?'

I looked at the turkey. 'Will you eat that poor creature?'

'Yes: it's healthy protein.'

'But science has proved that your body doesn't need meat in order to function in perfect health. As a matter of fact, many cancer-care organisations advise sufferers to give up meat and become vegetarians as a part of their treatment.'

She glanced down at the pale corpse.

'In buying that, you've already added to the demand for the slaughter of untold millions of animals each year.' She shuffled her feet. 'From the depths of my soul,' I said, 'I beg of you – please don't be cruel to animals. We progress spiritually through being kind to others. Respect the animals' rights and show them compassion. They're our spiritual brethren; and there, but for the Grace of God, go you.'

A cold breeze flapped her headscarf, and she became thoughtful.

'You asked about how to further your spiritual progression,' I continued. 'Well, that happens when we increase our awareness; when we cease to think only of ourselves and begin to consider the feelings of others.'

'Yes... I think I understand...'

'We can judge the state of our soul's evolution against many spiritual truths. And here's one of them: *those who would be cruel to an animal would be cruel to a human being.*'

'What exactly do you mean?'

'The *object* of the cruelty doesn't matter – the anger is inside the perpetrator.'

Dusk was falling fast around the bustling shoppers.

A flicker of realisation lit up her eyes. 'Yes... We just don't *think*, do we?' she said, quietly. 'We're brought up to eat meat, to buy furs – leather purses, shoes; to eat gelatine in food products. It's something we've always done, but... I can see now that just because it's tradition, that doesn't make it right.'

'This Christmastime,' I said, 'you could make a real difference. And in the new year, why not resolve to never again harm another being, including animals?'

Christmas decorations swayed high above us on the street lamps and their coloured lights danced over her face. 'Yes... I think I'll try.'

'That's good news. If we all tried harder to respect the Spirit of God which lives within everything, including animals, the human race would progress spiritually. Do you agree?'

'I do,' she said brightly. 'And after all, it *is* Christmas, isn't it?'

'Yes – and a good time to remember the Great Commandment that the Nazarene reminded us of: "Love one another, as I have loved you".'

We smiled and shook hands, wished each other the compliments of the season and she pushed her way through the people. I stood and watched her go until she became a blur amongst the snowflakes and the crowd.

But we'd parted company with much to think about.

My own thoughts were these: such a firm commitment to non-violence could be one of the most spiritual Christmas presents we could ever give back to God, as a token of our gratitude and reverence for the Gift of Life itself.

The choice is ours:
We can either kill, or care.

I'm no Angel but I've always stood up for
the underdog, and Digger was no exception.
I named the stray dog 'Digger' because he'd
suddenly appeared outside the flats where I
lived and had dug out a little dirt-filled hole
amongst some shrubbery for warmth. He
was a black-and-white (but mostly black
because of the dirt) Jack Russell terrier,
ever so timid, pathetic-looking and sad
when I found him.

'What's the matter, boy?' I said calmly,
trying not to frighten him. 'Haven't you a
home to go to?'

But he backed off warily, fearful and not
knowing what to make of me.

'Come on,' I said. 'It's such a cold day.
Here, sniff my hand first and then let me
smooth you. I won't hurt you, boy,' I
promised, reaching out my open palms to
him. But as soon as I moved forward he
belted away as fast as his little legs could
carry him, eventually stopping over the
roadway to glance back, half wanting
affection but terrified of human contact. It
was then that my soul-powers sensed his
psychic energy fields and I immediately

'knew' that the poor little chap had been badly mistreated – thrown from a fast car on the busy roads nearby.

I was both stunned and appalled by this cruel act.

But try as I might I couldn't coax him inside, so I decided on another course of action. Later that night I put out a saucer of milk and a huge plateful of Sooty's cat food for him. Sooty had glowered wilfully into my face and growled menacingly because I'd defiled the holiest of holies – her food dish. But I leaned over and stared right back into her bewilderment:

'Now, that's enough of that: we've got to be kind to Digger,' I explained. 'Some little boys have nowhere to sleep tonight, and no one to love them – not like you: you've got the life of Riley in this house, *and* the pillows on my bed.'

Grudgingly, she understood; at least I think she did, though two beady green eyes clamped themselves onto her food bowl, and followed it right down the steps and out into the cold winter night.

I was quite worried about Digger because when I retired he was nowhere to be seen and I just couldn't sleep; all I could think of was his dear little person, cold and lonely in the frosty night air. So I dozily got up in the early hours and went out to search for him again. Quickly yanking on my trousers and hopping down the stairs, grappling with a coat and flipping my slippers on, I crunched onto the frosty grass only to find that his milk bowl was empty and the food had all been wolfed. The poor dog must have been starving; not one morsel had been left.

Suddenly, in the moonlight, I caught sight of him in his little dug-out: it was only then that I had a good chance to get a close-up view, and his little ribs were sticking out through his muddy coat – he was so painfully thin.

But he wouldn't let me touch him: he quickly dashed off again into the night and stood firm across the road, glaring, waiting, hoping...

The weatherman on TV had predicted a bitter winter's night with temperatures falling to at least three degrees below zero. So I grabbed a couple of old thick blankets and a cardboard box, put them on the landing outside my flat (which was quite warm and comfortable) then coaxed the stray dog in through the front doors with promises of food and warmth, delivered in sympathetic tones. There, he gratefully enthroned himself in his cosy woolly bed and looked up at me with such grateful eyes.

On wishing him 'Goodnight', for the first time he allowed me to smooth his little frame, and as I did he licked my fingers as good as to say, 'Thank you.'

'God bless you,' I said. 'Sleep well, and we'll see what we can do for you in the morning.'

Before I closed my eyes that night I sought further help, turning to the Great Power.

I also asked the spirit people to help me find Digger a good home.

'Please don't let the authorities put him to sleep. Thank you, my friends.' And these were my final requests to the Other World.

But the next morning I got a shock: Digger was gone, along with his cardboard bed and blankets. The wicked old woman from the landing beneath me had thrown him and his belongings out into the freezing night; and the little dog – already so badly frightened and mistreated – was now nowhere to be seen.

I couldn't believe how cruel and selfish people could be.

When I confronted the selfish woman I let my feelings rip about her flint-like heart, to which she spat back: 'We don't want stray dogs untidying these landings. I'm not having that sort of nonsense round here!'

And there speaks the collective voice of the Children of Darkness.

Outside, the morning mist of dawn was pierced by the high-pitched whistling of the milk-woman arriving at our block. I greeted her with: 'Have you seen the little Jack Russell? I've been calling him Digger.' And I told her why.

'Oh, I wondered whose he was,' she said. 'He's awfully dirty and nobody's come to get him these past few days, poor little thing. He must be lost or homeless.'

'Can you help him?' I pleaded. 'I don't want someone destroying him and I've knocked all the doors and no one knows him.' She was obviously an animal lover; I saw her eyes blurring.

'I'll see what I can do,' she said kindly, which made me feel much happier about his fate.

And I wondered if my prayer was going to bear fruit.

Two hours later she was back with a car full of children clutching warm blankets and dog food. There was another puppy in the back, too, barking away as happy as Lassie.

'I've found him a good home!' she declared triumphantly – and I was absolutely delighted.

When she stepped out onto the pavement and smiled at Digger in his dug-out, the dog remained quite calm. She approached him, and this time he seemed to sense that salvation was at hand: instead of legging it, he didn't move a muscle – his little body stood firm. He just looked at me, then at her, then at the children and his new pal in the back of the car, as if to say, incredulously:

'For me? Have they come for *me*?'

I glanced back at him and smiled and nodded, as whistling-Annie lovingly scooped him up in a warm embrace. He wagged his tail so much we thought it was going to come off. I never thought I would ever see a dog smile – but I did on that day.

'Come on, my old son; you come along with me and we'll take care of you properly,' she cooed, folding him in a fluffy woolly blanket. (His grin was immense.) Then she smoothed his back, kissed him, cuddled him, put him in the car with his new playmate and whisked him away to a nice warm spot by a blazing fire, beside which sat a huge plate of proper dog food and doggy-biscuits, and a new life of friendship.

And from that day onwards the milk-lady and her family cared for little Digger, lavished love upon him, and called him their very own.

For months afterwards whenever I saw her I'd say, 'How's the dog, then?'

'Oh fine! He really loves us, and his new place. He's made loads of new friends and the kids adore him. He's got the life of Riley!'

'Just like my cat,' I laughed back. 'I had a soft spot for him, you know,' I said, 'and I prayed he'd find somebody like you to take care of him.' And we smiled at each other.

But each time I remember the day when Digger left, all I can see are his big brown eyes seeking me out and staring directly at mine as the car pulled away and turned the corner on that frosty morning.

His stubby tail was happily wagging away for the joy of his new friends, mightily strong for all he was worth. His heart belonged to them – but his eyes were mine, and saying:

'Thank you for caring, my friend.'

God bless you, Digger, wherever you are now...

5

Seance Secrets

Human beings belong to the animal kingdom and we share the same remarkable intuitive psychic powers that they possess.

We should never underestimate our natural psychic instincts. Our minds can 'sense', 'see' and 'hear' subtle vibrations of thought and feeling beyond the normal five senses. With practice, we can register the emotional atmospheres that surround people and the buildings in which they live.

Families radiate psychic atmospheres; so do nations, communities, social, religious, and political groups.

Just like our animal friends, who use these natural psychic senses to survive, we can learn to rediscover our own spiritual powers; and with these abilities we can communicate with souls who are now living in the next world.

But to make this contact more reliable, we must practice using these skills which seem momentarily 'lost' to modern man; I say momentarily because humankind has been here for millions of years and a few centuries are just an eye-blink in the vast scheme of time and eternity.

But until we can master these psychic and spiritual abilities we are bound to make many mistakes – all sensitives do.

Practice makes perfect.

Whenever two worlds are joined as one in a spiritual communication, the sensitive on Earth must direct his soul-powers and spiritual and mental energies to sense and see into the next world. On the Other Side of Life, the spirit people must do the same.

Communication is a two-way process.

It's a mind-to-mind contact, a soul-to-soul link.

So many delicate mental processes are at work when two worlds are trying to tune-in to each other, it's little wonder that spirit 'messages' can sometimes go 'wrong'.

These seeming failures have prompted me over the years to interrogate the spirit world about the art of communication, particularly about what goes on behind the scenes at seances.

Here, for the first time, is one of my many

spirit friends, my spirit teacher, White Owl, to grant us some fascinating insights which throw light upon, and answer many of, the intriguing problems involved when Two Worlds are blending as one.

White Owl:

This is how we in the spirit world perceive the events which happen 'backstage' at public and private seances:

Though audiences are aware of the calendar dates and times of my medium's work, we are not in this world, for there is no chronological (clock) time in eternity; but I pick up Stephen's thoughts of when a meeting is approaching.

We work with the language of Thought; telepathic messages are instantaneously flashed from mind to mind in my world, and some guides are able to transmit thoughts from one world to another, which exists at a higher rate of vibration.

When I am aware of service to perform on Earth, after my calls to a specialised band of helpers have been transmitted, I then delegate my current activities to other people and make my way down to Mother Earth. I home in on the frequency of Stephen's mind (for every soul has its own unique wavelengths within which its mind vibrates).

Sometimes we find our medium driving along a motorway or just waking up in some strange hotel after having had a long conversation with me in my world while his spirit had been travelling out of the physical body, at night.

Occasionally I find it necessary to remain beside my medium for the whole day on which a demonstration of psychic power is to take place, from the moment he wakes on Earth until the conclusion of our work together. It is not my function to protect him but rather to carefully monitor his mind and emotions so that when our time of joining comes I know what has affected him that day: how much stress, relaxation, tension, laughter, etc. All these expended energies can help or hinder our at-one-ment, and I like to be fully informed of his activities in order that I may provide the closest possible blending of our two minds at the point of contact.

Mediums activate their own natural auric-protection; their general character and inner motivation draws unto them persons from my world who are in attunement with these forces. The only fear mediums need have of attracting any undesirable influences stems from themselves: from their own life-styles, their own thoughts, feelings and true reasons for contact.

Motivation is the keystone upon which co-operation from my world is built, and *Like Attracts Like* is the Universal Law in operation at all times.

We can do nothing to alter or meddle with this power of attraction; the Law cannot be cheated.

We wait for attunement to take place at the meeting-point, but if our medium does not desire our closeness and refuses it, or is unable to raise his mind-vibrations to approximate to our frequencies, then we are powerless – and our influence will be unregistered.

In all the time I have worked with Stephen there have only been two occasions when an appointed meeting was cancelled. He was not at fault: once, his driver did not arrive, and the other time he tried to reach a venue through four feet of drifting snow but failed to make his destination. On both occasions I knew *before* he did that the demonstration would not take place; I foresaw the weather conditions and also saw his driver was fast asleep. I then immediately sent out thoughts to the spirit people who co-operated with the organisers in your world, and alternative arrangements were quickly made for different mediums to step into the breach: other sensitives were inspired by their own spirit-friends to attend and serve.

Through a strong sense of duty and loyalty to us over our years of service together, Stephen has earned our unstinting co-operation and trust. We are always there to serve, because he always is. *Like Attracts Like*: souls draw around them others similar in nature to themselves. If only all on Earth understood this.

When one sincere servant of the spirit steps forward to meet the needs of others, a thousand souls from my world step behind him, ready and willing to help. That is the Divine Plan: those who serve are served, and we will never fail our instruments, provided that they return our love and keep it burning bright with pure motivation based on the desire to spread knowledge and healing to mankind.

Now a few words about what occurs on Our Side during a public meeting.

Firstly, it is known to us beforehand who will be in attendance. We have access to a complicated network of interlinked thoughts and information, which can be tapped to discover who is likely to be present at the event. Though not an infallible system, it is very reliable, for everyone intending to come will have carried these thoughts in their minds for some time, and they are registered by trained people on Our Side. If, however, one of our projected recipients is *not* going to attend, then other spirit communicators are chosen and their relatives and friends on Earth are checked to see if they will be present. So one link replaces the other.

Ours is a very organised world: the power of thought is the quickest means of communication and, because of this, everything can be monitored faster than lightning speed. We do not just gather on Earth and hope for the best, there is a great deal of unseen order and activity behind working mediums. There are many souls on our side who lend their valuable services towards the success of a demonstration. It is not a haphazard spur-of-the-moment happening, but usually a well-planned and precisely actioned event, even though it can seem to be 'chaotic'.

Now a little about the spirit power and energies we require when joining the two worlds as one, for this is an often misunderstood aspect of our work.

Everyone who attends possesses an electro-magnetic field of energy — the aura — which is either vibrant with electrical impulses or sometimes (more often than not) it can be rather depleted. This accounts for the differences in energy between souls who are healthy, cheerful and optimistic, and others who are depressed and miserable.

So, to us — as far as our work is concerned — each person is a unit of fluctuating energy, a battery of power, each contributing to, or drawing from, the electrical atmosphere in the auditorium and surrounding areas.

When we are confronted with a thousand miserable and depressed people then the auric power available to us is considerably diminished. This can make our task much harder because we need to blend with human electro-magnetic impulses to aid our work. Black and turbulent thoughts (negative influences) impede our efforts.

What audiences contribute to public meetings is of vital importance to their success or failure. However, the medium is by far the greatest stumbling-block to our organised transmissions, as I shall soon explain.

If crowds do not emanate feelings of sympathy, kindness and attention towards Stephen then a great deal of their energies cause electrical disturbances in the auditorium which are unhelpful, and their auric power often becomes unavailable to us. If they are in grief, introverted, disinterested — or even bored and tired — their vital energies flow inwards, making them more difficult for us to tap. This can drastically affect the quality of demonstrations in much the same way as a transistor radio does not operate properly if its batteries are low. So it is with mediumship.

Audiences create — by the blending and mixing of their auric fields — a huge photosphere of electro-magnetic power (with other 'whirlpools of energy' moving within it) which is inside and often surrounding the meeting-place. When souls give their undivided attention or focus their minds on something outside of themselves, their energies flow outwards. Depending on the quality of this power our work is aided or hindered.

We sometimes convey this general 'power report' to our medium in his dressing room, before he takes the platform, particularly if conditions for contact are going to be poor. Along with his own sensitivity Stephen then obtains a reasonably accurate overall 'picture' of audience conditions, and whether or not the people will be co-operative or reticent to join in the spontaneous three-way spirit communication link, which, of course, is vital for the evening's success.

Stephen's own expansive aura can also be full of energy or adversely depleted, depending on his physical health and the peacefulness, or lack of it, within his mind.

When he makes contact with the public his sympathy and compassion (soul energies) go out to them. If the people are relaxed and comfortable with him then they are particularly receptive to his power and they quickly warm to his personality. This means that some who may have entered as cold and unresponsive beings will now — almost unconsciously — find themselves more at ease (because of interest in the medium) and hence they will automatically project and contribute more energy to the proceedings. They are now adding their personal power to his, and very often in his opening remarks we have heard Stephen say, quite correctly: 'According to what you give, so shall you receive.' This sums up the process quite well.

Without doubt, the greatest obstacle in any two-world communication is the medium. Physical tiredness impedes our thought-flows reaching him. If the body is nervously exhausted then it cannot function properly: the body only responds clearly to mental orders when it is fit and well.

But by far the most hindering of all circumstances is the medium's mind. If a sensitive is emotionally upset or clouded by psychological concerns, this sets up swirling energy-fields which can sweep away any of our subtle thought-forces and diminish contact with us. Instead of a peaceful, calm countryside scene where silence and harmony reign and everything is in a state of equilibrium and balance — this is the ideal mind – we now have to work through a mighty cyclone which is ripping through that tranquillity; and this is the mind of a psychologically-disturbed, mentally disquietened being.

The most difficult sensitives to reach are those who are just starting out on their development: they haven't yet established the ideal mental and emotional states of peace and balance which we require to obtain and hold a close rapport with them. These mental conditions are essential for successful attunement to occur. That is what psychic and spiritual development circles are for: to learn self-control and the stilling of turbulent forces which so badly affect our links with you on Earth.

Mediumship means attunement.

When successful attunement takes place, communication flows. When attunement is out-of-focus the receiver does not register us clearly. It is easier for us to reach mediums when they are cheerful, bright, optimistic, calm and mentally tranquil and also positively expecting success. But any fears or worries, anxieties and doubts — all of which create mentally-paralysing negative forces — and our clear links with them are seriously hindered. This is why sittings are unsuccessful in the presence of hostile minds. Those who wish to scientifically test the existence of us in Spirit must first look to their hearts before their intellect, their text-books or their own stony beliefs. Open-mindedness and sincere kindness are essential ingredients for successful communication to occur.

But let us now move on.

Seen by us, the meeting-place is of little importance and its walls do not entomb us as they do you; we can pass through them because we vibrate at a much higher rate than the physical atoms of the bricks. What we are conscious of is a vibrant pulsating electro-magnetic light, a vast battery of life-power upon which we may draw and with which we must successfully blend in order to gain good attunement.

Around the immediate area of contact a large band of helpers in my world is carefully gathering and assessing all the electrical, mental and emotional conditions, and is also speaking to people who will try to communicate later. But, although eager to relay their messages, communicators are not allowed to storm the medium: everyone is directed and organised and chaos is not permitted within the photosphere of sensitivity.

Through the generated power of our minds and auric fields — which we closely blend with Stephen's — communicators then step near to the medium and try to be heard, seen or sensed. If their attunement with his mind-frequencies is good then they are successful (usually in varying degrees). To aid this, around Stephen himself there is another sizeable group of spirit operators charging his electrical fields so that he stands within a highly sensitised sphere of energy. Communicators are then shepherded forward, one or two at a time. It is a very controlled process.

Neither are their messages off-the-cuff haphazard affairs, but they are usually quite well prepared. Communicators have been thoroughly counselled and reminded: 'Your loved ones in the audience cannot see, sense or hear you, but you must try to prove your survival. What can you say; what memories can you bring; what evidence could you give, or facts could you convey which would undoubtedly establish your presence?' They are also carefully advised to concentrate at the time of their transmissions and not to mentally 'wander away' or stutter incoherently — though some do just that, being emotionally overwhelmed at the moment of contact.

In the early days of our association I stood very close to my medium and acted as what we term a Control. It was my function to tune my mind so precisely with his that we almost became one individual. Communicators then expressed their thoughts to me, which were instantly registered by him. In the initial stages of a medium's development, while he is still learning to build his own sensitivity, very often he does not work directly with communicators but rather with spirit controls. These are highly trained experts in communication who take overall charge of the medium and his work.

There are also others present who monitor his health and vital physical systems while the mediumship is functioning. But once a medium's abilities are strengthened and well-established the controls step aside and the sensitive then works directly with the communicators on a positive mind-to-mind link. That is why people have sometimes remarked about Stephen's messages, 'It's just as though the spirit people are standing beside you. You make them very real.' To which he has often replied, 'They *are* very real.'

Because we are human beings and not automatons or machines, communication sometimes falters, breaks down or appears to fail. It is then my task to direct Stephen back onto the right track. I will often 'step in' mentally and say: 'You have made a mistake,' or 'Go back over it.' I have even had to tell him: 'Your recipient is lying,' when one man refused evidence we knew to be true.

My medium hears far more from us than ever he expresses, and that is because thought is lightning-fast, many thoughts are conveyed in the time it takes to physically vocalise one word.

Our mental links are sometimes so subtle and tenuous that it comes as no surprise when our connections to the medium suddenly break. There is then hurried activity here to do all in our power to re-establish solid contact as quickly as possible.

With so many varying conditions which can adversely affect our success we are always delighted when the meetings go well, for this indicates a good job of work has been accomplished. After all, mediums and guides have difficult tasks, delicate operations; rather like the fine tuning of a radio set into a transmitted station, the wavelength has to be just right. We can, and do, frequently miss our channels.

Because Stephen's abilities are now reasonably established (there is always greater unfoldment ahead, and no medium for the spirit world is ever fully developed), he works directly with communicators and often hears their voices as they were on Earth. Sometimes their language is none too polite! This, we believe, adds to the authenticity of the messages because he is often amused by what he hears and therefore spontaneously laughs. He is also sometimes emotionally moved by the deep poignant sadness as certain communicators remember their last moments on Earth, and this often makes audiences realise that what is taking place is indeed a very real process.

Stephen has always had a certain soul-empathy with others, even in childhood. This is a function of his Psychic Being in operation. His soul tunes-in to the person speaking to him and he becomes aware of a portion of *their* soul. If someone was in emotional pain he would feel empathy with, and sympathy for, him or her.

All good mediums are sensitive beings: it has to be so, or they could not be channels for the subtle and refined forces of the Spirit.

Those who don the mantle of service as prophets, seers, visionaries and mediums must expect their emotions and thoughts to become more acutely heightened. It has to be so; a human receiving and transmitting station — or medium — can only be in touch with eternity when the psychic faculties are sharply, finely tuned. And once our co-operators have discovered and unfolded their innate soul sensitivities they cannot ever lose them: they remain operational for ever. This is why we advise all mediums to cultivate tremendous self-discipline and a willpower of iron, and to master control of the self: a medium should ever be in full charge of his abilities, and not vice-versa.

It is the medium who 'tunes in' to our world (where we are waiting) — and the medium who 'tunes out' of our wavelengths.

We are not dictators, and you are not puppets dancing on our strings. It is always a conscious and willing co-operation between us, for our work is founded upon a mutual link of love, trust and service — not domination.

Behind Stephen, as he works, there can be upwards of eighty spirit helpers surrounding him at large public meetings. But there are also countless other spirits who come to witness demonstrations, too. They know they are not going to get a chance to communicate but nevertheless they remain in the vicinity to observe the powers at work. Occasionally they move unseen amongst audiences and perhaps stand by their special loved ones, trying to convey the thought of their presence and continued care and concern. This has prompted some of the public to say, 'Although I didn't get a message from the medium, I felt my people were there.'

The joining of Two Worlds can be an emotional, soul-stirring experience and it is not uncommon for people in both planes to weep when messages are being relayed. Their souls are touched. But of course there is also much laughter, too, especially when comical memories are transmitted, or when things go wrong.

Sometimes when two or three communicators are waiting near the sphere of sensitivity and one of them is unsuccessful — or recipients are unwelcoming — a new communicator will jump his turn and transmit a brand new link and, of course, Stephen receives it. This is a 'crossed-line' effect, when two messages are coming in at once. Not all spirit people are well-mannered. After all, they are human beings under emotional pressure and we have to make allowances. But through all this confusion Stephen must remain calm at its centre, and try to sort it out. Sometimes he has to start the link again until the lines are 'cleared'.

There have been times when we fully knew, before we even tried, that messages would go unclaimed by audience members. There are many different reasons for this, which I believe Stephen has written of, but the main one is *fear*. Thoughts of public humiliation or embarrassment also make recipients unwilling to participate. In Stephen's case all these fears are groundless, for he conducts himself with dignity in public. But audience fears make our work so very much harder than it already is.

After transmission, communicators often weep at the realisation of their success in getting, perhaps, only a few words through to those who love them; or if their links have been refused; or if they have not quite been accurately attuned and Stephen has not heard or sensed them properly. It is regarded as an experiment by my world, too; but communicators are not left comfortless. We take them aside, congratulate them, console them and speak about the joy they have added to the evening's events and to their loved ones' lives.

When Stephen is inspired to conclude the meeting, which often lasts two and a half hours, applause rings out in the theatre and we know our service has been appreciated.

But we are not always certain at this time just how much of what we have transmitted has actually been received by him and delivered to the audience. This is because we are concentrating on our medium as well as focusing on communicators and energy levels. (There are even doctors monitoring Stephen's heartbeats to ensure he is not overstrained or anxious. If he is, then they step closer and calm him by the power of their thoughts and inspire him to slow down and not to rush. There is a great deal of hidden activity out of physical sight.)

Afterwards there is usually a celebration on our side, a raising of joyous voices which makes every effort worthwhile, during which we have the inevitable dissection of the evening: not only by the communicators but also by our experts here. We are learning all the time.

We then leave Stephen's orbit and go our separate ways. We are not always beside him: spirit controls gather to perform specific functions and then depart until the next call to service.

No one in my world is at the beck-and-call of anyone in your world.

No one with you has the power to demand or command us to do his bidding; and we are governed by the same laws here. We cannot make anyone on Earth accept our teachings or inspiration.

Free will is a Universal Law.

After service, mediums often notice their personal power reserves have been drawn upon; and this is so. All mediums utilise their own energies when working with us. The physicist's definition of work is any activity which burns or expends energy. That is correct. In a medium's case the main loss of energy dissipates through the physical nervous system.

But the more power the audience gives, the less of the medium's own energies are utilised. All public demonstrators feel slightly tired after services simply because a great deal of power is burned up in their trying to convey meanings succinctly, as well as in physically conducting the meeting. It is very stressful to stand before a thousand people with nothing in your head except utter trust in the voice of the spirit, and a prayer that we will maintain our mental connections with you and prove our presence to the listeners.

The communications are 'live'; there is no script or rehearsal, it is all spontaneous; and it either spontaneously succeeds or fails. But we will not fail you.

It is my custom to remain close to Stephen for a short while after working, to inspire him to rest and get plenty of sound sleep, pure water, good food and clean air, for these are the constituents which build up the physical body and replenish the nervous system. I also impart some of my own power reserves to help him in these processes. His spirit will never tire, for the spirit is for ever linked to the eternal source of life, the Great Spirit — God — though the mind can sometimes become quite weary and in need of some tranquillity and a change of surroundings.

The great tasks upon which we in the Spirit are engaged, this work of spreading knowledge of an eternal life and all the deeper implications it brings in its wake, call upon all the physical, mental, emotional and spiritual resources of the human instrument. We feel extremely grateful and privileged whenever we link with mediums who have dedicated their lives to helping us preach the good news: *There is no death. You cannot die. You are as immortal as Consciousness Itself.*

To all Servants of the Spirit I say: never be downhearted or allow doubts to assail you about your magnificent efforts to spiritualise and enlighten mankind. You are representatives of the greatest power in the Universe — the Great Spirit of Life. You are His Ambassadors, carriers of the Living Light of the Spirit, a light that will ever guide you and never falter. Neither will it ever be extinguished.

We are here in your world to stay.

We need no church, no special creeds, no

certain race or person — but we will work with all those whose hearts are pure and whose minds are fixed upon helping mankind towards the discovery of eternal spirit truths.

Go forward then with love in your hearts and the desire to help all those who stand in spiritual darkness and ignorance of the truth, and we will step with you.

We will not forsake you, or leave you comfortless.

We are your friends and we love you.

We are attracted to you by the goodness and compassion in your hearts.

There is still much work for us to do: the harvest is plenty but the labourers are few. But if you will only co-operate with us, together we can change the world.

6

'O, Great White Spirit...'

*(White Owl delivers a public Invocation
prior to rendering service.)*

O, Great White Spirit,
Thou who art omnipresent and omnipotent,
the Great Mind Interpenetrating all forms of
life
and consciousness,
we raise thanks from our hearts and minds
for all Thy blessings which have surrounded us
this past week,
and right throughout our lives.

Gathering together in Thy name,
we wait within these sacred walls
to hold a service of holy communion between
souls
on Earth
and those in Higher Realms of Light,
this ground having been hallowed

by the Power of Love
generated by these, Thy Children.

Grace us now
with a mighty blessing upon our efforts
to bridge Two States of Being
with a clear and flowing link of Thought,
so that the Great Message of
Eternal Life
and
Eternal Love
may be proclaimed once more
by Thy Messengers of Light.

Silently have we come from realms of higher
consciousness,
patiently we seek Thy Spirit of Truth
that it may permeate our Thoughts,
Words and Deeds.

Most Gracious Spirit,
Mother/Father Principle,
we cannot help but be mindful at this time
of all Thy Children,
in all Thy Kingdoms,
who feel so bereft of compassion in their lives;
those who feel neglected,
lonely, comfortless and afraid,
believing that the very light of their days

has been extinguished by the darkness of grief,
personal loss,
or the stifling powers of hate and ignorance.
Grant us, we pray,
further strength that we might hold aloft
a Torch of Truth,
to light a new way for them;
so that they may know they are
openly Loved,
secretly Guided,
and ever Supported
by the strong hands of Ministering Angels,
both seen
and unseen.

O, Great White Spirit,
just as You have never forsaken
any of your Earth Children
(not one)
especially at their times of greatest need;
so shall we stand always in readiness
to render Service to them
through You.

All we ask in this Great Work
which we have undertaken
to help spiritualise the Universal Family
is that the Inspiration,
Guidance and Courage
will flow unabated

from the Wellspring of Eternal Light,
until the glorious day dawns when
Peace reigns in the Souls of all Your People,
in every World of Consciousness.

We also now transmit
a special Stream of Thought
for the Animal Kingdoms on Earth:
that Man may come to Love them
as he ought to Love himself,
and give them the respect he should show
to his Brothers and Sisters.
May the time come soon when these,
Thy Gentle Creatures,
are set free from oppression
and the cutting chains of cruelty
which have been locked and fettered on them
by Mankind.
May their innocent blood be spared.

Universal Father
and Mother,
Unfailing Guiding Light,
bathe us all now
in the Radiance of Your Wisdom.

And accept from me,
One of Thy many humble servants,
my heartfelt thanks;

and those of this man through whom I speak
(my Earthly friend) —
and also the sincere gratitude of these,
Thy People, who have gathered here tonight
in the name of Eternal Love.

May Peace be ever with us:
Surely, so let it be...

7

Spiritual Healing Powers

*Health and Peace
through the Natural Laws*

Psychic power can manifest in many different ways and one of these is through the power of spiritual healing: *we can heal ourselves*.

I've lost count of the correspondents from around the world who have asked me the questions: 'How can I gain peace of mind? How can I be healed?'

Peace of mind, and I mean *true peace and tranquillity within the mind, body and spirit*, automatically brings in its train a beneficent and mighty power of spiritual healing energy, which may correct all kinds of illnesses on all levels of being.

Mental and physical peace are essential ingredients for health. Where there is harmony there is wholeness; where there is disharmony there is disease of one sort or another. If you can gain perfect balance within your body, mind and spirit — you will gain health.

There are many ways to attain this healing peace of mind, but one of the simplest is to use the psychic power of sound vibrations.

Because we are spirit beings, in essence the same as our Father/Mother God Creator (who is a Great Spirit) we can draw upon the vast well of powerful spiritual vibrations which are all around us.

In a moment I'll suggest a simple self-healing exercise for you to try, but first let's take a look at the vibrations of music and the positive psychic effects that they can bring us.

When we hear the sounds of a beautiful melody our minds are soothed and calmed, and our spirits are lifted out of this mundane world and into realms of peace and tranquillity.

Such is the psychic power of music.

Down through the centuries, music has moved and inspired us, and refreshed our bruised and battered souls because *the psychic vibrations of sound radiate powerful healing forces.*

All around us the great rhythm of Nature is rather like an orchestrated healing symphony: dawn's peace, night's thunder; evening rain and morning birdsong, all these are parts of a majestic musical score which represents the Great Pageant of Life.

But before we attempt to draw upon such 'hidden' healing energies let us first recognise that sound is Ether in vibration. *Everything that exists is in a state of constant motion; every thing in this Universe is continuously vibrating.*

Life is Movement.

Physical objects (including our bodies) are composed of protons, neutrons and electrons which are constantly circling so fast that they give our eyes the *illusion* of being solid matter; but, in fact, they are nothing more than an open network of vibrating energies.

Furthermore, each object emits its own unique high-frequency psychic sounds. The Universe itself radiates a general vibration which approximates to the sound *Ah-um*, as many eastern religions know.

Devotees chant *Ah-um* in an effort to 'program' or 'raise up' the vibrations of their minds and bodies to more closely 'attune' their souls to what they consider to be the God-Vibration.

All objects vibrate the ether at specific

wavelengths; and our souls do this, too. We each project into the atmosphere around us a spiritual and electro-magnetic life-energy-field called the aura; and we each generate our own unique *Auric Note* or fluctuating *Key-Sound,* which is created by the vibrations of our thought patterns and emotions, and also by our state of spiritual evolution.

Such 'hidden' psychic energies are constantly being exchanged all around us.

Think for a moment of a thunderstorm: when two electrically-charged rain clouds meet, the higher-charged mass sheds its power to the lower, resulting in a magnificent display of lightning.

Even the chairs we sit upon supply us with similar but more subtle energy exchanges; but it is by an act of purposeful will that we can attract more of these cosmic energies towards us.

When we quieten our thoughts, our inner psychic bodies can more actively absorb these energy-boosts from the environment: from other souls, from trees, radiant sunshine, clean air and pure water; and even from the psychic atmospheres inside buildings – certain of which can also adversely affect us.

(If you doubt this, when next you feel

depleted sit in a dark and drably-painted brown-and-black room and see how these low-frequency colour-vibrations will depress you even further.)

But to substantially *increase* your personal battery of life-energy and spiritual healing power, why not try this simple visualisation exercise, whenever you feel the need:

♦ First, set aside some special time for yourself, when you know you won't be disturbed.

♦ Next, select your favourite meditative music, something soothing and calming – nothing excitable or brash. Play some soothing, pleasant music; slow classical or meditation music; or perhaps birdsong or other sounds of the natural world.

♦ Then lie in a semi-darkened room, close your eyes – and listen...

♦ Quieten your mind and relax.

♦ Breathe deeply six times: the very air itself contains hidden cosmic life-energies known to the ancient mystics as *Prana*.

♦ Further relax your body and mind by

mentally or vocally instructing them to 'slow down', 'become calmer' and 'be tranquil, and at peace...' until you have gently coaxed yourself into a state of perfect relaxation.

♦ Breathe deeply again, six more times. Draw the powerful *Prana* in the air right down into the bottom of your lungs until you feel your abdomen rise slightly with the downward pressure of your diaphragm.

♦ Be still, and enjoy your music. 'Blend' with it and 'float away' into its soothing vibrations of sound.

♦ To help you to succeed: try to 'picture' the sounds as any bright shade of your favourite colour: see them washing over you in waves, interpenetrating every part of your spirit, mind and body.

♦ Or visualise the sounds as invisible waves of radiant power, undulating towards you, engulfing you; and 'breathe' in these spiritual healing energies as if they were air.

♦ If you are a religious person, you may wish to pray at this time or send out

requests for help to the compassionate
spirit friends who watch over you.

♦ You could even project healing energies to
people in need, everywhere: they will
receive them because distance is no
obstacle to spiritual healing power.

♦ Do this exercise for ten to fifteen minutes.

♦ Breathe deeply, six more times... Relax;
then open your eyes and return to
normality.

Try it, and see.

The symphony of Life itself is full of
cosmic power; but we must remember that
great musical pieces also contain some
discordant notes. In addition to the pure
harmonies which are linked to the key
signature there are other sounds which can
momentarily disturb or jar our senses, but
they soon resolve back into the original key.

Only after the music is over do we realise
that these discords have deepened our
appreciation of its beauty. They have made
the experience more emotionally stirring
and joyful.

Life is like that, too: it's a wonderful

experience, but it also has its discordant times.

Once we realise that our souls and minds are in a ceaseless state of vibration and energy-flux, we can appreciate that we are continuously generating our own unique Soul Vibrations and projecting them into the Universe around us, constantly adding our pulsing thoughts and emotions to The Great Power, as well as drawing our life-sustaining energies from it.

This raises an interesting question: what kind of psychic 'music' do you project into the world around you?

What song is *your* soul singing? Is it a healing, harmonious melody, or a painfully discordant one? Does it enrich the lives of everyone, or disturb their sense of peace and well being, as well as your own?

Is your life a song of unconditional love, compassion and service? Or does it resound with selfishness, hatred or other negative forces and therefore make you suffer from some form of dis-harmony or dis-ease?

When your time on Earth is done and you cross over into the light from whence you came – how you will be remembered?

In the meantime, however, while we exist here on the Earth, as sensitive people we must learn to survive in a materialistic world. But how can we live healthier, more peaceful lives in this modern world which bombards us with constant stress?

Is there some method or some strategy which may bring us peace?

Yes, there is.

Those who are gifted with the power of clairvoyance or 'second sight' and who can see the soul-world and the energies it radiates, know that spiritually developed people are relatively free from stress. They shine out from the centre of themselves a psychic aura of healing tranquillity; and these people can bathe our tired minds and bodies in the life-giving waters of cleansing love.

But how can we, ourselves, become as peaceful as they are?

Well, it's been truly said that we can only express *outwardly* what is already present *within* us. Someone whose mind is stilled and uncluttered by disharmonious and negative thought-energies, who carefully chooses polite speech and is never garrulous, and whose actions are only those of a kind and helpful person, is well on the way to mastering the mind and emotions and obtaining peace. Such characteristics mark these people out as spiritually evolving souls.

And we can join them. We can make a closer connection to the mighty peaceful God-Power which is within us by entering the silence.

According to ancient mystical schools, God (the One Mind which created All) dwells in utter peace and stillness. The Spirit of Consciousness which fashioned every manifestation of life exists at the back of, and is also expressing Itself through, all of Its outward Forms. Yet paradoxically It dwells alone in the Great Silence.

It isn't surprising, therefore, that people whose minds and personalities possess not only a depth of genuine tranquillity but also a fuller expression of unconditional love are sometimes regarded as God-like beings.

People who are advancing spiritually are radiating into the atmosphere around them the invisible yet living soul-lights of God's peaceful love because they possess a greater recognition of, and attunement with, the Great Healing Power.

'By your Light you shall be known.'

And we can be like these people if we express more compassion in our lives. I would define a compassionate soul as a person who is so aware of, and so in sympathy with, another soul's distress that he takes immediate action to stem or alleviate his brother's suffering. This is kindness in action; active compassion of the highest order.

But there is also another important quality which we will need to develop before we can attain perfect health and peace. It's a characteristic about which many sensitive people often remain unaware; and it is this: *the vital need to generate within themselves their own powerful healing battery of soul-strength.*

No sensitive person could possibly survive the stresses and trials of life in the twenty-first century without a well-disciplined mind: mental strength is a vital part of any soul's spiritual armour.

Without inner strength our spiritual harmony can be easily upset by the noise and clamour of a world which often grates upon our responsive nervous systems.

Unchecked, our thoughts have a tendency to gallop out of control like wild unbroken stallions. In order to achieve and maintain inner harmony, health and peace — and therefore a state of happiness and well being — we must learn to rein in and control the wild horses of Thought, or nothing but chaos will rule our lives.

Mastery over the mind is one of the goals we must achieve if we are to progress spiritually.

The mind should be man's servant, and not his master. The mind should be man's healer and not his destroyer.

If we neglect to develop a strong will power, our resolve to walk self-chosen and often testing spiritual pathways can falter and sometimes break.

We must learn to be strong: the generals in the army of the Spirit must not run away at the first sign of battle.

Today, millions of people around the world will wake to greet the sunshine and they'll feel reasonably peaceful and content. If you are not one of these souls then maybe it's time to change your thought patterns.

There are a number of natural laws which, if we try to understand them and then apply them in our daily lives, will help us to gain peace. And there are also some basic guidelines which can help us to achieve a happier state of mind:

We can start by recognising that happiness is an outlook; an attitude, a way of looking at and dealing with situations.

To achieve balance and harmony in our triune nature of body, mind and spirit, we must learn to welcome with fortitude and positivity the many challenges which life on Earth will present to us; and then do everything in our power to overcome them and win through.

To advance spiritually, we must grasp 'the beast' of our lower selfish nature and tame it through the power of our will, until it becomes 'the angel' of our compassionate higher self.

Happiness and contentment bring health; and it is not so much what happens to us that matters – what counts is how we deal with it.

To achieve contentment is not easy. But then anything worth possessing must be spiritually earned, diligently worked for:

Take some time each day to still your mind, to draw upon the inner soul-healing spirit which is your very life-force.

In your quiet meditation times, think about your problems carefully and try to solve them.

Periodically cleanse your mind by releasing past hurts or regrets. The past is gone and you can't change it.

Forgive and forget.

Move on.

How can you embrace the future with open arms if your hands are clinging on to the past?

You can't.

And remember the important Natural

Law of *Cause and Effect*. Spiritually, we will receive from others precisely what we have sent out into the universe in the past (and perhaps even in past lives).

So start each new day with fresh hope and a more positive attitude to life: try smiling again.

Be kind and thoughtful.

Be considerate to everyone around you; and gradually you will feel more content.

As we have sown, so shall we reap.

Many people bemoan their circumstances and claim they don't deserve the lifestyle they endure because they say they've never harmed another soul.

But this is not true.

Actions and Reactions are equal and opposite; and if we are spiritually honest with ourselves, we'll acknowledge that we are receiving now only what we have earned through our previous actions – that is the Law.

Divine Justice rules this Universe and everything is known to The Great Mind.

And here's another important law which will help us in our quest for health and peace: the law of *Personal Responsibility*.

We alone can change our attitudes; we alone must resolve to be happier souls.

We can be advised by others, certainly

(and this guidance and inspiration is always available); and we can be supported in our efforts – but the task of changing our outlook, and therefore of improving our health and well-being, is ours alone.

Once we realise that all life is spiritual in essence and that physical matter is nothing more than a temporary shadow cast by a much greater Spiritual Light, we can see that the surface of existence is like a furious ocean where huge waves of constant activity break against everything in their path, including us.

But spiritually aware souls can stand firm against these storms because their feet are firmly planted on the ocean bed, deep down in the depths of peace, where the absolute calm, stillness, and power of God reside.

And it is from The Great Spirit that we can draw the unlimited healing strength and inspiration which we may need in order to deal with life on Earth.

A well developed, balanced spiritual personality resembles a fine silk thread: it possesses sensitivity and responsiveness to the multifarious vibrations of life around it – and yet this seemingly delicate spiritual thread is as strong as flexible steel wire.

So: where do you stand on the road of

spiritual development and health and well-being? Are you weak-willed and likely to lose your sense of peace to the slightest stress or misfortune that befalls you? Or do you possess a strong and determined mind which has the sensitivity and firm resolve to muster all the love and healing strength within it so that you can face each new life-challenge and conquer it?

Do you radiate and express the Peace and Love of God in all that you think and do?

Are you a kind person?

The answer to the question 'How developed is my spiritual nature?' must surely be: 'There is much more progress ahead of me.'

By looking back on our lives we can see how the pattern of our soul progression has gradually emerged over the years; and we ourselves dreamed and formed this design within our younger minds.

The years have rolled onwards and we have certainly evolved: we have developed as personalities, expanded our awareness and formed moral codes.

But although the children that we once were are no longer visible, somewhere deep within the psyche they are still 'alive' and prepared to surface sometimes when we least expect it.

But I do believe we owe a great debt to those youngsters, for it was they who formed our present lives out of their childish dreams and hopes.

Since my earliest years I've always been a bit of a daydreamer, which made me feel as though I was 'lost' on this planet.

As a child I felt as if I were a stranger here, a changeling who had come to Earth; a being whose mind and spirit floated high in mental clouds but whose feet were firmly held in clay.

But there's no doubt that my childhood dreams are responsible for what I am today: and I would say that the same law applies to you – to everyone; for yesterday's dreams are tomorrow's realities.

Little Dreamer

dream your dreams
   little dreamer
wrapped around in velvet sleep
breathing deeply through repose,
an angel crowned with golden curls
   playtime's over
   and night unfurls
   her dark blue robe of starpoint lights
dream on
   little dreamer

snug beneath pink-quilted sheets
so warm and soft and tight
then float away into blissful sleep
and leave the blackened night
far behind you —

    to sail the tides of time and space
    in a sailboat made of paper lace
    entwined with silver threads of light:
    onward through cloud-mountained night
    into the land of peppermint dreams
    past flights of dragons
    your dreamboat gleams,
    manned by a soul
    who dreams and schemes

and way up there on the cloudbank's height
floating free and rushing like the wind
you'll plan your little plans
and set tomorrow's course
with your rudder in your hand

and then fly high
  little dreamer
over the milky seas so white
through rising waves of uncertainty and doubt,
flapping the flag of masterplan
and shining brilliant hope-lamps
(that'll never go out)
as your paper-lace dreamboat rocks and sails
through all the pictures of your ancient past,
and all the future roads your life entails

then go skim the verdant trees

becoming the spirit of the breeze
that beats the cornfields as you fly
  soar high
   little dreamer
  soar high:
   circling the air in your paperwish boat
   and building tomorrow within your soul –
for come the sunrise, you will inwardly know
the magic that'll free you
     free you
      yes
      free you!
   from a dull drab workaday world,
   and you'll see a new beginning:
     new hopes
     new pathways
     as yet unfurled

but now set a new tack and sail away,
kissing a sunset glorified,
over cliffs of conscious thought
and sinking back to mother earth
   where then
   little dreamer
you'll awake, my child –
leaping and laughing, you'll arise!
    dancing on earth
    what was skipped in heaven
    deep in the realms of a midnight sky

night-time travellers
grow up to be
  little dreamers
  like you and me

so dream your dreams,
don't set them apart –
remember them always
and lock them in your heart

For this evening's flight is tomorrow's reality
and twilight hopes are sunrise actualities.

*

*No one can possess
the Whole of the Truth;
we each have a small portion of it;
not one of us knows
the entirety of
Absolute Truth...*

8

The Burning of the Witches

Visionaries, mediums, prophets, sensitives and spiritual healers have had narrow-minded religious bigotry hurled at them for centuries.

Regrettably, and to the great shame of Christianity, history reveals that in The Dark Ages the early Christian Church led an enthusiastic crusade against countless psychic sensitives and tried to extinguish the psychic light from Earth. Behind these actions was a Bible text that reads *'Thou shalt not suffer a witch to live.'*

Many Biblical scholars regard the origin of this phrase as unclear and it's now widely thought to have been a latter-day addition to the text. Nevertheless, it seemed to grant the early Christian church absolute power to maim, imprison, torture, persecute and burn to death countless healers, psychics and mediums for fifteen hundred years or so.

It's impossible to place an accurate figure on those who lost their lives but it surely must number in the millions.

'Witchery' was said to be possessed by individuals who, by any means other than practices acceptable to the established Christian Church of that time, healed the sick, saw visions of the future, found lost objects or persons, or conjured up the spirits of the so-called 'dead'. These acts were pronounced evil and linked to the Devil and his adversaries, whereas, in fact, all these psychic abilities are perfectly normal functions of the spirit body and are exercised by naturally sensitive people.

Today's Spiritualist Church still actively encourages mediumship within its religious ceremonies, gifted sensitives being allowed to conduct public services and relay spirit communications via their gifts of clairvoyance, clairaudience and clairsentience (clear-seeing, clear-hearing, or clear-sensing of the presences of loved ones from the Next World). It's all so naturally delivered and it's often a beautiful, dignified and simple service to witness.

But despite the sincerity of many mediums, since early in history it seems we poor sensitives have never had an easy time of it. A case in point is that of the world's most famous psychic: The Maid of Orleans — Joan of Arc — who heard spirit voices which guided her to lead the French Army to triumphant victory in battle.

Her supernormally-heard voices angered the Church of her day, but even when she was under threat of agonising torture she refused to deny their existence.

The Church was exasperated by her sincerity and in 1431 at Rouen it applied the afore-mentioned text and accused her of 'sorcery and heresy'. She was but nineteen years old when pronounced guilty, chained to a stake and burned to death — watched, it's claimed, by more than 10,000 people. Afterwards her blackened and charred remains were then thrown into the River Seine.

Poor Joan.

She was, and always had been, a devout Catholic girl and witnesses claimed she uttered forgiveness to her ecclesiastical accusers even as she died. As the flames destroyed her youthful body, the last words issuing from her lips were said to have been: 'Tonight, by God's grace, I shall be in paradise.'

But it took 477 years before the Christian

church officially beatified Joan of Arc in 1908; and two years later in 1920 she received the honour of sainthood.

Such tragic trials and persecution of the psychically-gifted continued unabated for centuries. On British soil, in Scotland, the story of Bessie Dunlop from Lyne in Ayrshire is another case in point.

It was in 1576 when Bessie was accused of being a witch and then burned alive, mainly because people claimed that near her 'the voices of the dead' were heard to speak. Bessie was obviously one of those rare and gifted individuals who possessed what we now know as Physical Mediumship. A physical medium is someone in whose presence the spirit people may manifest in a complete or partly complete temporary physical body. In Bessie's case the communicators would have constructed, by thought, a 'mask' made of special bodily fluids and plasma — known today as ectoplasm — which would have been withdrawn from the medium and others in the vicinity. Into this they would then have pressed their vocal organs and hence been able to vibrate our atmosphere and speak. Bessie Dunlop was what we now call today a Direct-Voice medium.

Paranormalists have long understood

these wonderful phenomena and there have been many books written about them, notably an informative array of writings by the historian and Spiritualist writer Arthur Findlay. Two of his excellent titles are *On the Edge of the Etheric* and *The Rock of Truth* (Psychic Press Ltd) both of which are worthy of serious study.

Such powerfully-gifted sensitives like Joan of Arc and Bessie Dunlop are indeed rare individuals who, because they stand apart from the crowd, are misunderstood by people with little or no real knowledge of how psychic gifts work.

The last 'witch' may have been burned in England in 1712 but even in modern times sensitives have still not escaped trial and punishment, mainly because British law was set against the practice of mediumship since the inception of the two archaic 'Witchcraft and Vagrancy Acts': 1735 and 1824 respectively. Under these, sensitives could be prosecuted and 'suffer imprisonment by the space of one whole year without bail', for the 'pretence' of 'witchcraft, sorcery, enchantment or conjuration' or even for claiming to 'tell fortunes'. Incredible as it seems today, especially when one thinks of the long lines of palmists at popular seaside resorts, the prison sentence was implemented in the case of modern-day Scottish medium Helen Duncan, on 3rd April 1944.

Helen was a Spiritualist and a powerful physical medium in whose presence the 'dead' fully materialised themselves in temporary physical bodies (constructed of the previously mentioned ectoplasm). Her abilities were tested and proven genuine many times.

The police arrested Mrs Duncan while in a state of deep trance during a seance in Portsmouth. Such violent action towards a sensitive in a heightened nervous state is always dangerous — in her case this caused her to haemorrhage; nevertheless she was still charged under the Acts and later sent for trial at the Old Bailey in London.

And even though nearly forty witnesses testified on oath that their loved ones had physically appeared to them, spoken with them and kissed them during Helen's remarkable seances, British law allowed no real defence for it simply didn't recognise the existence of genuine mediumship under the two archaic Acts.

Mrs Duncan even offered the judge and jury a courtroom 'test seance' so that they might witness her exceptional psychic talents for themselves but —

'What really matters is that man learns
to live at peace with himself and others...
The message is far more important than the messenger.'
Stephen O'Brien

A smile and a wave
for the people in the theatre circle.

'I was thunderstruck as I beheld the form
of my former self – me,
as a boy of six years old.'

Adam Taylor, aged five, who died after open heart surgery, contacted his parents at a Manchester meeting. They later wrote: 'We thank you from the bottom of our hearts for the comfort we have received by getting proof that our son lives on in another place.'

Stephen with his Tour Manager, Jeff Rees Jones, sorting through one of the many boxes of fan mail at the Voices Management offices.

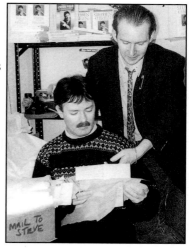

Stephen with some of his youngest fans at a W H Smith book-signing session.

Early morning queues waiting to enter the Wembley
Conference Centre, London, where Stephen was to make a
guest appearance. Over two thousand people attended.
(Photo: Ray Taylor)

A quick dust-up for the bright lights and TV cameras.

Stephen relays a spirit message to one of the many thousands of strangers who attend his meetings each year.

Stephen O'Brien. 'God, who dwells in silence, knows I've always tried my best. He will send me His strength. He will not let me down.'

incredulously — this was denied, and she was found guilty of 'pretence' and imprisoned for nine months.

But her imprisonment was not the result of purely religious and legal bias: political motives could have been involved. In one of her materialisation seances during the Second World War, a young 'dead' British sailor returned in a fully-materialised body to tell his relatives that he had lost his life with many others when his ship *HMS Hood* had been sunk by enemy action.

Members of the public had now heard of this ship's sinking *before* the War Office had received official intelligence reports of it.

Spiritualist writers alleged that Winston Churchill had recommended Mrs Duncan's imprisonment because she was obviously a threat to wartime national security, particularly as secret plans were already underway to accomplish the D-Day landings and the British government was fearful that these, too, might become known.

Helen Duncan became known as 'The first martyr of Spiritualism' and since her death there have been a number of campaigns to clear her name.

Until the Witchcraft and Vagrancy Acts were more or less 'replaced' in 1951 by the 'Fraudulent Mediums Act' — a much fairer statute which at least recognised that genuine psychic phenomena can occur — the police would often stand at the back of public meetings and sometimes arrest the medium.

Times have changed, thank God, and nowadays we live in a far more civilised, open-minded and educated world. But thankful though we sensitives are that we're no longer burnt alive, I'm afraid we're still occasionally tortured — mentally, of course.

Even though we're in the New Age of Aquarius, it's incredible to think that some sensitives are still publicly vilified — and I'm no exception.

In June 1990 I took part in a discussion on a television show that was transmitted 'live' to millions. A middle-aged and bespectacled Reverend David Holloway represented the Christian Church. Why on Earth the media still encourage the clergy to criticise paranormalists completely baffles me. What has mediumship — the fact that communication takes place between two different states of being — got to do with orthodox religious creeds and dogmas?

Communication has little to do with faith — it's a psychic science: a fact, not a belief; it occurs, whether we choose to believe in it or not.

Anyway, let battle commence:

Holloway: It was quite clear when Christ came on Earth that there were manifestations of evil. Now I don't believe that a lot of what goes under the name of Spiritualism or mediumship is all genuine. Some of it is bogus, some of it is fake. But there clearly are occasions when certain things happen which are true — but, the Bible makes it clear that we're not to dabble in it.

Presenter: Is it dangerous?

Holloway: I have to say that I believe it is. Some of it doesn't seem so, necessarily, at the beginning. I mean, it's a bit like drug addiction. I mean, you may start with marijuana or something that's innocent and then you gradually go down that line. I mean, a lot of it is very, very innocent...

Presenter: So presumably, the more you do it the more chance you have of getting into sort of, serious difficulties?

Holloway: Yes, I mean, I would say, of course, as a Christian I believe that Christ is greater than any of the forces of evil and therefore there's release in Him.

Presenter: Well, we have with us tonight, Reverend Holloway, one man who — if I might say — has done it many times before. If I'm not mistaken, Stephen O'Brien, you've contacted some 30,000 people, I'm led to believe, who are on the Other Side, as it were: you are a medium. Who is it, or what is it that you make contact with?

Stephen: I make contact with the minds, the spirits, the souls, the personalities of people who have live here in this world and have now finished with this world and gone into what one man called 'The Kingdom of Heaven.'

Presenter: So in that particular —

Stephen:—There is life after death.

Presenter:—yes, and so you agree with Reverend Holloway?

Stephen: No, I don't agree with everything he has said. (*Now addressing the clergyman*) First of all I would like to say to you I think that the viewpoint you've put forward is very narrow because Christianity is not the only religion, in this country or the rest of the world. There are Buddhists,

Mohammedans, there are Spiritualists. Spiritualism is a state-recognised religion registered at the Home Office, with its own ministers. They are ordained; they can conduct naming services, marriages, funerals, and — in many cases — don't get paid for it like the Church of England do.

Holloway: ... Yes, but, I mean I would have to say that ... I agree, of course... there are other religions... but as a Christian I believe that Jesus Christ is the way, the truth and the life; and one of the things he came to do actually was to destroy the works of the Evil One. Now, again, I'm not willing to sit in judgement on anybody, but the question is: 'What is truth?'... And, um... one of the reasons why I'm Christian is because I do believe that Jesus Christ rose from the dead on that first Easter Sunday morning... But what he did was, he made it quite clear, through his apostles, that we're not actually to deal with this sort of thing.

Throughout the above, at no point did I say or even imply that this clergyman's belief was similar to 'drug addiction' or that it may have been linked to 'the works of the Evil One', nor that it could be 'bogus' or 'fake'. However, he levelled all these accusations at my calling.

I find that very sad.

It's also worth noting that most of the world's respected spirit guides agree that today's Christian Church has strayed so very far away from its origins that the Beneficent Power of God — the exercise of the Living Gifts of the Spirit — can no longer can find a dwelling-place within some of its walls or, more importantly, in the hearts of many of its people.

But in antiquity, contact with eternity was a reality for the early Christians, as the following startling extract from an ancient book proves. It's taken from *De Anima*, believed to have been written in 211 AD by a Roman lawyer, scholar and early Christian called Tertullian (AD 160-230).

For seeing that we acknowledge spiritual charismata, or gifts, we too have merited the attainment of the prophetic gift. We have now amongst us a sister whose lot it has been to be favoured with sundry gifts of revelation, which she experiences in the spirit by ecstatic vision amidst the sacred rites of the Lord's Day in the church. She converses with angels, and sometimes even with the Lord. She both sees and hears mysterious communications. Some men's hearts she understands, and to them who are in need she distributes remedies. Whether it be in the reading of the Scriptures, or in the chanting of psalms, or in the preaching of sermons, or in the offering up of prayers, in all these religious services, matter and opportunity are afforded her of seeing visions.

After the people are dismissed at the conclusion of the sacred services, she is in regular habit of reporting to us whatever things she may have seen in vision, for all her communications are examined with the most scrupulous care, in order that their truth may be probed. 'Amongst other things,' says she, 'there has been shown to me a soul in bodily shape, and a spirit has been in the habit of appearing to me, not, however, a void and empty illusion, but such as would offer itself to be even grasped by the hand, soft and transparent and of an ethereal colour, and in form resembling that of a human being in every aspect.'

This was her vision, and for her witness there was God, and the apostle Paul most assuredly foretold that there were to be spiritual gifts in the Church.

This woman was obviously a practising medium: she was a gifted psychic, healer and clairvoyant who used her abilities to serve the people of her faith.

Tertullian exhibits far more courtesy, intelligence and common sense than many modern-day clergymen when he states that the medium's utterances 'are examined with the most scrupulous care' to find any truth in them. It's also noticeable that the woman's inspiration wasn't ignored or pronounced demonic and evil, neither was it immediately alleged to be 'fakery' or 'against God'.

Over two thousand years may have passed, but fundamentalist groups have picketed several of my meetings — and even one of my book-signing sessions. The police had to be called to disband the chanting protestors because they were hassling the public and denouncing my book as 'the Devil's Word', a phrase to which I take objection because my work is accomplished through the Power of Love. My work is all about spreading knowledge of the truths revealed to us through spiritual experiences. I try to bring comfort and hope to people; I believe in God, too — and all roads lead back to the same common Source.

Yet, despite this, many of you will know I've been spat upon, derided, ridiculed in private and in public, and in the media by certain Christian Fundamentalist groups — none of whom knew me personally, or had read my books or witnessed my mediumship. If they had, they would have known of my deep respect for the man Jesus and for his life and work.

'Love ye one another' is not only a tenet I've always upheld but also one I've tried my best to live by.

Like Joan of Arc, I stand by what has been revealed to me.

I will never deny the existence of my voices.

For decades I've relayed thousands of spirit messages from all kinds of people who came from all different walks of life — even from 'deceased' members of the clergy.

We will all survive death, no matter what religion we profess to follow; even atheists and agnostics survive. It's also been my experience that clergymen have sometimes startled their relatives with their spirit communications.

I recall one deceased vicar who contacted his beloved sister. After relaying convincing evidence of his survival, he certainly gave her something to think about.

'I'm OK over here, Margaret,' he said. 'But there's something I have to tell you. I wasn't met by our Lord.'

'Then who *did* meet you?' she asked.

'Mother and father; and my son, Tommy. And there was no sleep until the Resurrection Day, either. I was up and about the moment after my heart attack.'

'I see,' said his sister, rubbing her chin thoughtfully. 'Is there anything else I should know, Derek? Is there anything you want me to tell the family?'

'Yes, my dear. No one can remove from us the mistakes we have made. There is no vicarious atonement, Margaret. We have to work out our own salvation. It's been a great shock to me. When I think of all those years I spent travelling, preaching the creeds and propagating the dogmas of my Faith... I feel now that I want to atone for my "sins".'

'Have you met the Lord?' she asked with keen interest.

'No, my dear. He's such a great spiritual master that He's far in advance of people like me who've just arrived here. Though I do hope to meet Him one day when I have progressed more.

'Meanwhile, I shall stay close to you all; I shall try to inspire people with the important part of the Christian message: that we should try to love and forgive one another; and live in peace together... But

Margaret — I'm so sorry for all the other wrongs which I taught.'

This man's sister must have questioned her faith very closely after receiving such a staggering revelation.

And here's another example of a priest's spirit-return with an unusual message — but this time he was accompanied by a nun and he communicated at a large charity meeting in which I appeared. The event was filmed as part of a regional television programme and it raised hundreds of pounds for blind and deaf children.

The following extract is taken from *Psychic News*.

When Stephen O'Brien took the platform he linked a war veteran with a relative in the audience. 'His name is William,' said the medium, 'he sailed on *HMS Victorious* in World War Two, but returned unhurt.'

'That's right,' agreed the relative.

Stephen continued: 'He's telling me "We sailed near to Folkestone Harbour".'

'Yes.'

The communicator then referred to the two houses he had left when he passed. 'The settlement will take six months,' added Stephen. 'Does that make sense to you?'

'Yes, it's right.'

Stephen then described Aunt Lizzie,

dressed in old-time music hall costume complete with a feather boa. 'She was in amateur operatics,' he explained.

'She was,' agreed the recipient.

'And she sings here *My Old Man said Follow the Van*. You're moving house?' This, too, was correct.

'You've paid a bill for £60,' Stephen told a young recipient.

'Just this minute,' she replied.

'Your great-grandmother is telling me about this,' Stephen explained, and she says, 'I'm Mary Jane.'

'Oh yes, that's her name!' answered the delighted recipient.

'She says you're thinking of marrying soon.'

'I am.'

'Mary Jane is telling me "He's a good-looking boy. Tell her I approve".'

The recipient's stop-gap method in dealing with a minor crisis was revealed when Stephen announced, 'You've just laddered your tights and made a quick repair job.'

'I tied a knot in them,' confessed the girl to the audience's amusement.

A Protestant and a Roman Catholic returned to one woman: 'I'm the Reverend Harries, looking for Mrs Rees, one of my flock,' said a clergyman. When Mrs Rees was located he added that he had officiated at her family's services.

'That's right,' agreed the woman.

'And he's brought a Catholic nun with him — Mother Maria,' added the medium.

'I knew her well,' replied Mrs Rees.

Stephen then explained there was an unexpected visitor with the clergyman: 'About thirty years ago he christened a stillborn baby boy in your family, signing the cross in water on his forehead,' he said. 'He's brought the boy with him but he's now a grown man, of course.'

This unusual message was accepted by Mrs Rees.

Another woman in the audience recalled the vagrant hunchback who returned to demonstrate his survival to her. She agreed with Stephen's statement that she had lived near a school when she was young.

'This man slept rough near there,' added the medium.

'I remember him,' she replied. 'I recognise your description.'

The poignant message from the communicator was, 'Thank her for smiling at me.'

Now let's finally sweep away the incorrect assumption that spirit communication is a modern-day development which has suddenly surfaced under the in-vogue title of New Age Practices.

Here's a very interesting quote from a man who was born about one hundred years before Jesus walked this world. He was a Roman statesman, orator and respected intellectual called Cicero (106 — 43 BC) who wrote of eternity and frequent contact with it. But then, the spirit world has always been with us; men have walked and talked with 'Angels' (translated directly from the Greek as 'Messengers') since time began:

> They whose minds scorn the limitations of the body are honoured with the frequent appearance of the spirits. Their voices have been often heard, and they have appeared in forms so visible that he who doubts it must be partly bereft of reason.

Here endeth the history lesson.

9

Two Worlds

Here's an interesting article which was one of my several contributions to Two Worlds magazine, founded in 1887 by Spiritualist pioneer Emma Hardinge Britten.

I've written on many paranormal topics but after that last chapter I thought I'd like to share with you this story involving the spiritual teacher, Jesus, because it conveys a powerful message to all those who claim to follow or represent Him on Earth.

Waiting for the Master
A Tale of Love, Re-told

The old widowed fisherwoman was very excited as she fussed around her humble kitchen near the shores of Galilee. She tidied and meticulously swept out each of the tiny rooms which were her home, merrily singing away to herself as she went.

Her mind was so full; she could think of nothing else but the wonderful news she'd heard. A great and noble Teacher was to pass through her village sometime that day: Jesus was his name — and many had called him a mighty prophet and seer.

With each sweep of her brush she convinced herself that without doubt it would be she who would receive an honoured visit from him. He would stop and rest awhile at *her* home — she was sure of it. She'd prayed so hard for it to be so; and her great faith made her strive all the harder. She wouldn't be found with an untidy house.

As dawn blossomed into mid-morning she wiped her tired brow and ran to the foot of her garden where she leaned over the creaky gate, searching the horizon for her special visitor. But he was nowhere to be seen.

Just then, her eyes fell upon a wizened thin washerwoman whose back was bent under the weight of the huge basket of wet clothes she was carrying. The old lady laid down the heavy load, stopped at the gate and said:

'I've walked so very far on my shaky legs, all the way from the stream in the valley.

Please, I'm very hungry. I don't wish to be any trouble but could you possibly spare a crust of bread that I might eat?'

'Oh I'm so sorry,' said the fisherwoman, 'but I can't stand at the gate all day — I've such a great deal more work to do before my guest arrives. You'll soon be home, old woman, and then you can cook a grand supper for yourself. But please call again when next you come from the stream.'

And the fisherman's widow scurried up the path into her house, leaving the hungry washerwoman to trundle up the steep hill towards her own place, where there was no food in the larder.

By tea-time the house was spick and span, but still there was no sign of her guest — and the busy woman feared that the Master Teacher had passed her by. She fretted and moaned: 'I've missed him. But he *must* visit me. I've cleaned my house from top to bottom and warmed it especially for him.'

All at once there was a knock at her back door and her heart leapt up for joy. 'He's come!' she exclaimed. 'He is here!'

But on opening it she saw only a poor ragged boy with no shoes on his sore feet, and she noticed the blue veins standing out on his thin frame. And she felt so sorry for the lad.

'Please,' he pleaded, clasping his hands, 'I have no family and I've walked many miles, so very far since dawn: could you spare me a small piece of fish or perhaps some water or wine?'

Although her kind heart went out to the boy she was aware of time swiftly passing; so she explained how busy she was and promised that if he came back the next morning she would milk her prize goat and give him fresh fish and bread to eat. And she slowly closed the door.

Then she dashed around to finish her off chores in preparation for her guest. But by night-time there was still no sign of the Master; and all at once she began to reel, her mind falling into dark despondency and fearing that she really had missed him or that he'd passed her humble dwelling and had visited a wealthier hearth than her own. Then there was a sudden noise — a scratching at the wooden door.

She jumped to her feet, elated, and in a surge of joy she ran across the room, unbolted the latch and swung open the door: only to find a wounded stray dog looking up at her mournfully. Its paw was badly hurt and bleeding and its eyes were full of want and homelessness.

'Oh you poor thing,' she said, gazing

pitifully at the creature, recognising its need for warmth and sleep. But her business-sense grasped hold of her and she started to panic, suddenly remembering she'd not yet made up a new straw bed for the Master. So she said to the dog:

'You may sleep outside by my barn tonight, my friend, and I'll dress your wounds and feed you tomorrow when I have more time.'

She latched the door and made up the Master's bed. After this she slumped into deep depression and disappointment at being overlooked by the Teacher, who had not come. Utterly exhausted, she lay down on her soft warm bed and fell into a deep sleep...

Then, in a vision, the Master stood before her.

His form was glowing with golden rays.

'Oh!' she cried in delight, 'My Master! I thought you'd forgotten me!'

'No, my child,' replied the Teacher, 'I did not forget you. *Three times today* I knocked at your door and begged for your help. And *three times today* you turned me away, without the love I needed.'

*

10

Dear Stephen...

When all's said and done, what matters most is that we respect each other and try to help one another. There are many times in our lives when we all need some comfort and encouragement.

The following handful of letters are just a few of the many thousands I've received from around the world. They show just how much a spiritual message can dramatically affect the lives of ordinary folk who receive evidence of survival or knowledge of the spirit world through it.

Normally, I'd have removed some of the compliments but I ask your forgiveness because I think the impact of these simple and yet profound personal messages can be conveyed only by the writers' full comments.

I hope you'll agree; and here we go:

Dear Stephen,

I am writing to thank you for the communication from my late husband, which you gave me from the spirit world.

You asked was there anyone that had 'links with Swalwell, and with an old gentleman?' Well, my late husband and I used to visit an old gentleman at Swalwell and had many wonderful times with him.

You then went on to describe my late husband, and said he was 'pointing to the left eye and laughing, saying "Do you remember the fun we had?"'

My husband had a slight cast in his left eye, and at times he would tell our son, John, that because of the cast the eye was loose!

He would place his hand over the eye and pretend to put it into his hand.

When John looked for it, he would pretend to drop it and John would spend quite some time searching the floor!

You also went on to say about 'tummy pains' my daughter was having, and that my husband advised me 'to have her seen to as it isn't what you think it is', being her age.

Well, she attended a local hospital and sure enough she needed treatment, and is now fine.

Many thanks Stephen, for your wonderful

work. Kindest regards —
  Mrs T
  Washington

Dear Stephen

After seeing you at Winchester I just have to write to you.

Can you remember me? I am the lady who had a communication through you at the end of the evening.

My dearly-loved brother came through with the following facts:

He took his own life by locking himself in his car in the garage of his home last December 26th.

He attached a hosepipe leading from the exhaust through a rear window and sealed it, so the fumes filled the car and poisoned him.

He said he was sorry, wasn't in his right mind at the time, and now he was happy with his son X on the Other Side.

The work you do is so important. God will bless you for all the comfort and hope you give to so many people, and, like many others, I pray you will be blessed with good health and strength to carry on.

  Yours sincerely
  (name and address supplied)
  Hampshire

Dear Stephen,

I believe you will be interested to know than an appointment made by Spirit, through you, was kept.

I attended your meeting at Southampton where you brought my father to me and gave accurate evidence. At the end of the message you said, 'Your father says he will be with you on 25th August'.

I suddenly remembered I was booked to go to Stansted Hall (Arthur Findlay College of Psychic Studies, in Essex, England) for a week, on the 24th August. I was taking my mother with me and we would be in the Sanctuary on the Sunday 25th for the usual service there.

The 25th arrived: after a beautiful service, the clairvoyance started and Margaret Pearson (the medium) asked if anyone knew of someone just about to go in for open heart surgery. I physically felt a push in my back (from the spirit world) and I put up my hand, as only two days before a friend had told me that her husband had been called by the hospital. Superb evidence was then given to me, and then Margaret said 'I have your father here', and he proceeded to talk with my mother and bring back lovely memories, all exactly correct.

I was asked to tell the full story during one of the lectures that week, to show that indeed Spirit can make appointments, and although we have free will they are certainly aware of arrangements we make, and can plan to be there.

All good wishes for your continued work with Spirit,

Sincerely,

Mrs M M

Hythe

Dear Stephen,

Where to begin?

You visited Tunbridge Wells, Kent, and the first message you came through with was from a very talkative, very urgent little boy of eight years old called 'Ben'. Dear Ben, despite his meagre years, managed to 'muscle' his way to the front on that night!

Ben, as you accurately described, 'was hit by a car on his way to school, crossing the road'. As you described, 'the damage was all to his left side and he was blind in one eye'.

His parents, who are my next-door neighbours (and dear friends) are people who you would describe as 'the salt of the Earth'.

I gave his mother Ben's message and it brought her overwhelming comfort. I cannot express in words how much!

His mother was able to verify all the names you gave, etc, and she was relieved that 'he felt minimal pain', because she had feared this.

How can I begin to express what one can only feel? Ben's communication through you has brought sunshine back to the lives of two very special people.

God bless you, Stephen.

J: (name and address supplied)
Surrey

Dear Stephen,

I am a psychologist engaged on research. May I say I was very impressed with your work tonight at the Lewisham Theatre, London.

I deal with the laws of probability and tonight the evidence you produced would stand up to statistical significance tests. You have nothing to fear from investigation, and nothing to gain.

Yours sincerely,
A T
(Research Psychologist,
full name and address supplied)
London

Dear Stephen,

Last year I was fortunate enough to see you on stage at Watford. The first lady you called out of the audience, unbeknown to me at that time, was coincidentally my friend's

Mum, whom I did not recognise, even though all the evidence that you gave her about her son in spirit matched up.

Afterwards I told her daughter about it and she confirmed that it was her Mum.

As you may be aware, the sceptic critics really tried to pull you apart in our local newspaper, but her Mum wrote to them and they published her letter which stated that she was most certainly not planted in the audience.

I have seen many mediums but have never heard so much proof in all my life; you were spot-on.

Congratulations on the wonderful work you are doing.

Yours sincerely,
Miss J
Watford

Dear Stephen O'Brien,

I felt had to write to you saying how much I enjoyed reading your books *Voices from Heaven* and *Visions of Another World*. I was moved to tears many times reading every word on every page.

I have to say that these books have changed my life in so many ways. I have learned that the things we all worry about from day to day, and the things that we let upset us, are not so important after all.

They have taught me that the most important things in life are love for mankind, and richness of thought and spirit.

If people who put all their time into making money and who are wrapped up in their own selves could see what the other side, and the spirit world, was like, I am sure we would put less importance on material gains.

There are many people in the world who, if they wanted to, could help many other people improve their standard of living.

God bless you, Stephen,

Good health.

S P

Kent

Dear Stephen,

You have helped me so very much, I thank you with all my heart. As with your first book, your second book just jumped out at me off the bookshelf.

I don't really know how to put into words how your books have made me feel.

They have made me laugh, cry — so many things I have felt, but I think most of all they have helped me to find me.

I thank you once more, Stephen, for what you have given to me, and so many others. May God bless you always.

May your work of Love carry on for many

years to come.
  God Bless You,
  Yours sincerely,
  Mrs S M
  Peterborough.

Dear Stephen,
  I admire your work greatly.
  I have always feared 'dying', but after reading your books and attending one of your meetings, I find all my fears have gone.
  Thank you so much, Stephen.
  Take care of yourself and keep up the good work.
  Best wishes,
    Mrs C A
    Hants

Knowing about my spiritual healing work, which is mainly done through the power of prayer these days, this next lady came to one of my meetings hobbling on a crutch. Her arm was in a sling, too, but she dismissed herself from hospital to attend.

Dear Stephen,
  Hi! I don't know if you remember me, I was the girl who came up after the Norwich show and had had a motor-cycle accident the previous night. This will probably sound

stupid but when you gave me a hug I felt such a surge of absolute Love rush through me, it was incredible.

The most unbelievable bit about it all was that all evening my arm had been hurting quite a lot, but by the time I got home and went to bed, it hardly hurt at all. AMAZING.

Thankyou
VERY MUCH
  Lots of Love,
  Helen T.
  XXX
  Norwich

Dear Mr O'Brien,

I'm very pleased I attended one of your evenings at Carlisle. Although I wasn't fortunate enough to receive any communication from the next world, I was deeply moved and so very pleased for those who did.

I want you to know that this has brought me so much comfort and I no longer feel so alone. I no longer fear death, for I know there is no such thing.

Afterwards, when you were signing your books, you asked me what I'd been doing, for I was walking with the aid of a crutch. I told you I'd had multiple sclerosis for twenty years. You mentioned spiritual healing; I'm very interested in this but don't know of any healers in my area.

Finally, Mr O'Brien, thank you so very much for coming to Carlisle and for showing me, along with so many others, that there truly is life after death. Thank you for sharing your wonderful gift and for the caring way you convey all the messages from the spirit world.

I wish you peace and happiness, and hope that you continue to bring peace to those who are grieving; on both sides, for many years to come. God Bless You.

J P
Cumbria

Note: Spiritual Healing can be transmitted across continents and worlds, distance being no obstacle to the soul-powers used. While every effort is made to help patients, healing should always go hand-in-hand with medical treatment delivered by qualified doctors — ultimately, of course, all lives are in God's hands.

The Harry Edwards Sanctuary is a world-renowned charitable organisation which undertakes much commendable voluntary work in this direction. For help, write with a stamped addressed envelope to: The Harry Edwards Spiritual Healing Sanctuary, Burrows Lea, Shere, Guildford, Surrey, United Kingdom, GU5 9QG.

For Details of the address where you may write to Stephen O'Brien for help, please see page 351.

11

Questions and Answers

The public avidly thirst for knowledge and although I've discussed a wide range of spiritual issues in my previous books, still they want more. Over the years I've been asked to comment upon hundreds of psychic subjects.

Here, by public request, is another varied selection of my answers to some fascinating questions on the paranormal.

Is there sex after death?
If you wish it. Most experiences can be duplicated in the Next World, except the formation of physical bodies. Physical bodies are created from physical matter for specific use in the physical world.

In all worlds every activity is mentally perceived and experienced, and therefore can be recalled and reproduced.

What is the purpose of sex?
It's the means whereby two physical bodies multiply the species. But the soul comes from the Great Spirit.

How would you explain hermaphrodites: people with the outward appearance of both sexes?
This is simply a genetic peculiarity. Their inner essence, the soul, is the most important attribute.

Is it possible for a person of one gender to feel they've been born as the wrong sex and therefore feel trapped in the wrong body?
Yes, I think so. Memories of previous lives or powerful present-day desires play a large part in this. Some spirit teachers tell us that we've lived many lives and therefore we have previously incarnated as either sex.

So when we die, do we remain male and female? What is the sex of the soul?
The soul is genderless. What matters is the mind, the experiences, the evolution, the thoughts and feelings. Each incarnation adds maturity, depth and understanding to the whole being.

Some say that practising mediumship affects a person's sexual balance. Would you agree?
Not entirely, but the working of the psychic or soul powers certainly does affect the body's nervous and hormonal systems.

Some teach that female mediums accentuate their masculine characteristics, while males enhance their feminine qualities.
I think there's some truth in that, but it's not entirely due to the mediumship. Women taking public meetings have to call upon their stronger, more positive side to get them through the ordeal. Men, on the other hand, like the women, must express the love of the communicators and it's not easy to prevent this affecting your delivery.

We must remember that mediums of both sexes are sensitives in all senses of the word and we shouldn't get caught up in the stereotyping of individuals. Bodies are only temporary physical coverings, it's the soul that matters; and that, in essence, is both 'negative' and 'positive', or 'masculine' and 'feminine'.

Is it wrong for two adults of the same sex to love one another other?
How can love be wrong? If two people

genuinely care for each other and share
their lives to the mutual benefit of each,
then those experiences will obviously
benefit them.

*Then why do some people condemn these
relationships as 'against God', 'evil' or
'perverted'?*
Because they're narrow-minded people who
are ignorant of the true nature of God —
the Universal Laws. Bigots of all
persuasions believe only *their* thoughts are
'right'; and you can often recognise them by
their loud voices. (*Applause*)

*Do the planets affect our characters and
destinies as in Astrology?*
Everything in the Universe influences
everything else to greater or lesser degrees
because all life is interconnected. It's well
known that the Moon's gravitational field
affects our tides and also, some claim, the
fluids in our bodies.

Regarding astrology, if you're speaking of
the tabloid press columns advising you not
to cross the street or you might meet
someone in a red coat who'll upset you: no, I
don't accept that.

Neither can I accept that because of
certain planetary positions our lives and

characters will be shaped. The vibrational fields of the universe at the time of our birth will probably have an effect upon us but not to that extent, for the soul is eternal and when we're born the constellations are actually being viewed as *pictures of the past*. Light takes millions of years to reach us, so when viewing the night sky we're actually seeing the Universe as it used to be, not as it actually is now.

The most important thing to remember is that whatever influences are around us, our human spirits can triumph supreme over any obstacle which challenges them.

We are the masters of our own destinies and there is no force so great that it can remove this right to govern our own lives.

Is there intelligent life on other planets?
Yes, there has to be. Think of the billions of stars and planets in our own galaxy then in millions of other galaxies, and then in Universes beyond these.

Statistically there's bound to be life elsewhere and the Spirit World confirms this: there are planes of existence (other worlds) far ahead of us intellectually, and others which have yet to reach man's status.

Have you ever spoken with God?
Yes, every day. God is Infinite Mind, a Consciousness permeating all levels of Thought and Being throughout the Universe. We speak with God in everything we do.

Have you ever seen God?
Every day. All things animate and inanimate are manifestations of the God-Force: you are, so is a flower, a child, a stormy sea and the bright shining stars. We can only see the manifestations of God.

Have the spirit people seen God?
Yes, but not in the way you might be thinking. God isn't a man. The spirit people, like us, are aware only of the Creative Mind's manifestations.

Why do you think we've been born on Earth?
To develop our souls, to hone the character and to experience further conscious awareness of who and what we are. Earth is a growing place and no perfect beings have ever incarnated here. Here we may progress physically, mentally, emotionally and spiritually through meeting challenges, which mainly stem from our inter-relationships with others.

The world's people are so cruel and selfish, I feel it would be so wrong to have a child and make it suffer.
But *your* child might be the one to change all that.

Are any New Souls ever created?
The soul, or rather the spirit that motivates it, is ancient. There has never been a time when we were not. Our mind-force or Primary Essence of God has always existed, but it's only in this present characterised state that we're conscious of our current identity. So when we talk of old and new souls we should remember there's nothing new in this Universe. It has a wonderful way of re-cycling itself: energy changes its form continually but it springs from an ancient power.

What is Soul-Affinity?
The mutual attraction of one soul for another or for its group-soul.

What is a group-soul?
Several individuals — sometimes on both sides of the veil — joined as a group and working together because they belong to the same frequency or wavelength of soul

213

evolution.

Like attracts like whether we're on Earth or in Spirit; and the power of attraction is Thought: motivation and feeling. We're all part of various group-souls, all independent yet interconnected at one and the same time.

What is recognisable as your self in this physical life is just the tip of a vast iceberg; by far the greater portion of your Mind exists beneath the surface.

My sister was pregnant and tried everything to abort the foetus but her son was born healthy. Why?
Because where a soul is to come into the world it cannot be stopped.

But what if she'd been successful and lost it?
Then the child would have been born elsewhere. The soul comes because its spiritual blueprint dictates it.

But then it would have different parents and a different upbringing.
It seems so, but not in the deeper sense. Souls choose the circumstances whereby they might progress. Time is of secondary importance: if one opportunity passes another will soon present itself.

214

There's always a Divine Plan at work even if, at first, we fail to perceive it clearly.

You say the spirit body leaves the physical after death, but I've heard we have several bodies. How many do we have?
At death we pass into the Astral Plane, those worlds of Thought nearest to the Earth, there to express ourselves through a spirit body which will eventually dematerialise to reveal another vehicle of expression beneath it.

As we progress onwards into higher planes, spirit teachers tell us that rather like shedding the skins of an onion we shall inhabit many more spirit bodies, which are within us.

If we've lived before, why can't we remember who and what we were?
Because when taking on the flesh there comes a cloaking-down effect which often obliterates many memories. The physical brain is far too simple a computer to register the entirety and vastness of the mind.

You maintain there's no such thing as possession, when one soul from the next world totally controls another person in this world. Can you prove this?

I'll try to explain:

Each night billions of people go to sleep then move out in their spirit bodies into the Next World. When they return in the morning, why hasn't somebody else 'possessed' their bodies while they were away?

It doesn't happen because your spirit blueprint, your mind, soul and body are all intricately woven to make the one and only Being which is you.

Your body is yours, it comes under the direct control of your own mind and spirit and no one else can assume that role.

What about your guide when he entrances you? Surely he's possessed your body?

No, because trance operates in varying degrees from the light and almost imperceptible to the deep and cataleptic. But even in deep states it's still a close impression of the mind, not a domination.

The medium's spirit is close by and co-operating. Trance is a blending of personalities and minds, rather than an annihilation of the medium's right to govern himself.

I've sat for nearly forty years in a psychic

development circle and never experienced anything profound. Why is this?

Either you've been trained incorrectly or your psychic abilities are so deeply buried within your soul that they're not ready to surface yet.

But forty years haven't been wasted; your soul will have become more sensitive and if you view your unfoldment more objectively, you'll be surprised at the progress you've made.

Flowers only bloom when the seasons are right. Likewise, soul unfoldment can't be rushed.

There's no such thing as instant soul attainment.

Why can my cats and dogs follow my deceased relatives around the room when they visit me, while I can't?

Your pets should be up here taking this meeting! (*Laughter*) Animals are usually far more sensitive than humans are; their psychic perceptions are much more acute. A dog hears frequencies of sound way beyond our physical capabilities.

Do the spirit people remember everything, or do they write it down?

They're quite fallible like us. They have

217

books in the Next World. In fact, there are vast libraries of works in every known and now-extinct language. They have copies of all Earth publications there; places to study them in and special ways of permanently recording events for future reference.

They most certainly don't know everything. I recall several occasions when audience members at my meetings have informed their communicators on the Other Side that a friend has just passed over, only to get the reply, 'Oh, has he crossed over to us? I'll do my best to locate him.'

Why do some religious people condemn your work as being 'of the Devil'?
Because they're steeped in ignorance and trapped by superstition and fear. (*Spontaneous applause.*)

Empty vessels make the most noise.

Why do you think some sections of the popular press misrepresent the life and work of mediums?
Because they often print what they think the public wants to know, not necessarily what the public would really like to read. Some newspapers are only concerned with circulation figures and coins chinking into the bank. These publications will 'dig up the

dirt' on anyone they can find.

I would caution you all never to accept as the absolute truth anything you read; God gave us minds to think matters out for ourselves.

Why are people allowed to die in earthquakes?
No one 'dies' before his or her time, and earthquakes strike because the planet is evolving just as we are. Those people are there for a purpose at that time of tragedy.

My brother was stabbed to death but his murderer hasn't been caught. What will happen to the man who killed him when he dies?
He'll receive his judgement. Judgement is automatic: the soul moves into the spirit world for which it has fitted itself according to its acts, thoughts and deeds.

In the same way as a fish can only live in water and not on land (because it can only exist in its correct place), so does the soul move into a sphere of life that it's earned for itself during Earth-life. The soul finds its own level.

The murderer, like everyone else, will inherit a keener mind on passing into the next world, a sharper memory and perceptions that will make him aware of broader viewpoints. Then there will come a time when the pain he inflicted on your brother will disturb his conscience and, one day, he'll have to face your brother. After this, the 'wrong' will have to be made 'right' by the murderer, usually through service.

A medium brought a message from my father in the next world and Dad mentioned his own birthday. You teach there's no calendar time Over There, so how did he know it was his birthday?
He must have picked up your thoughts: they don't follow the clock or the seasons in the Spirit World so that's the only way he'd be aware of his anniversary. Thoughts are living things, and our loved ones are only a finger-touch away, you know.

Have you ever been on stage and received no spirit messages?
Never — but I've struggled through very difficult meetings when the contacts were tenuous and quite unclear.

There are over 1,500 people here tonight; let's imagine each person brought in ten relatives or friends with them from the Other Side, which makes roughly 15,000 communicators. A few of these are bound to have some degree of success, as long as the medium is properly attuned to register them, of course.

Why don't the spirit people give you their full names and those of the people they wish to contact?
Many do, sir, but I'm not always sensitive enough to hear them properly.

On good nights when reception's clear I've received full street names and addresses as well as other precise facts. But linking two worlds together is never easy which is why every attempt should be viewed as an experiment.

A thorough investigation should be made before reaching any conclusions about whether or not life is eternal.

My grandmother was very shy. Would this prevent her from communicating tonight?
If her desire is great enough nothing will stop her trying; but forthright personalities tend to push their way to the front.

I've been to a number of good mediums but my husband has never sent me a message, and he died twenty years ago. Why is this?
There could be several reasons:

He has no desire to communicate.

He's tried but been unsuccessful.

He might prefer to speak to you at night when you're asleep and out in the spirit world beside him.

Or it might be against his beliefs.

Keep investigating and giving him as many opportunities as you can to reach you, perhaps by regular visits to a Spiritualist church where communication occurs at most public services.

Is it right for mediums to make a living off the backs of the bereaved?
Oh, I think you've got your wires crossed there: you're talking about undertakers, not mediums. (*Applause.*)

Everyone at this meeting has chosen to be here to share this spiritual experience. (*More applause...*)

* * *

Here are some interesting questions and answers taken from various sources, but this time they touch upon more personal themes:

Do you have a steady relationship at

present?
Yes, with myself. I've tried the other kinds and learned you can't find happiness outside of yourself. It doesn't reside in other people or objects: it's within. The most important relationship we'll ever have is the one we have with ourselves. Every other is secondary.

Even before one with God?
Of course. If you haven't found yourself, you'll never find God. If a man doesn't know himself, how can he ever hope to understand others? And if you can't find yourself, how on Earth can you find God when the realisation of God is within? You can't — it's impossible.

Do you live alone?
No, I live with my cat and I'm perfectly content. Some people need others constantly fussing around them for comfort and emotional security to avoid being lonesome. I don't. Those kind of emotions probably stem from man's past evolution — the herding instinct.

I don't need that kind of attention. It's often stifling, demanding and unnecessary.

Is that because you're an independent

Aquarian?
Well, I'm certainly independent — and Aquarian.

People can let you down, so I've moved away from too much dependency on others.

What are your thoughts on marriage?
For some, it works and can be a fulfilling experience. But as far as I'm concerned, we're all individuals and it's impossible for a piece of paper to spiritually bind people together. As long as respect exists in a relationship, it's worth preserving; but once that's gone, it's over.

You didn't mention the word Love.
That's because true Spiritual Love never dies, but the kind of 'love' that some couples share is nothing of the sort.

What is it then, in your opinion?
Oh, it could be many things: infatuation, physical attraction, lust, admiration, or an emotional insecurity compelling you to seek company. There are many different reasons.

Then what's the purpose of marriage?
If you mean the purpose of relationships: to develop as minds and characters through shared experiences. So many partnerships

divide because one person outgrows the other on any of these levels. But it's a soul-growth process.

Your psychic talents: are they gifts or abilities?
Both. God gives the gifts, but it's our responsibility to develop and unfold them.

Have you perfect faith in your psychic abilities?
When they work well, it's marvellous.

But when they don't it can be quite disappointing.

I wish I had more control over the conditions that make mediumship function at its best, but I don't. There are too many conflicting factors involved, mostly connected with the public and the spiritual atmospheres they project into the auditorium.

What's the biggest problem with your public work?
There are two: lack of clear reception from the spirit world and unresponsive crowds. The more psychic energies the audience gives, the less my own are burned up; the less they give the more tired I get, which makes the results much poorer.

If more people learned to give instead of take, they'd get much better results at public demonstrations of mediumship.

What's the biggest problem in your private work?
As far as the sitters go: the biggest stumbling-blocks are cast-iron minds which demand specific details, or hostile personalities who are not really listening to what I'm saying.

As far as the medium goes: his or her emotions and mental disturbances can impede communication. Tiredness and ill-health deplete a medium's psychic energies, too, making contact harder to get.

Do you fear death?
No; death is a friend.

Do you fear facing huge audiences and having no messages to give?
No; but it wouldn't please me. I take the platform to succeed, not to fail.

You've often spoken of leaving the cities. Why?
Because sometimes they depress me: masses of people all functioning on different levels of existence — moral, spiritual and

evolutionary — and they can radiate coarse psychic vibrations.

People can be very irritating and sometimes I need to get away from them, to exist in silence.

I've always tuned-in to my surroundings; that's just the way I am. Loud and aggressive people repel me. Very few people radiate peaceful and positive healthy thoughts — the opposite, in fact.

But in the country, next to nature, great psychic energies soothe and heal my spirit and I need these in my life.

But surely the cities have good souls in them, offering compassionate services?
Yes, but compared with the selfish masses they're relatively few.

When you were a boy you said you felt ill-at-ease in this world. Why?
I was a changeling; a dreamer, an idealist — a child who didn't seem to fit into his family. I once thought I was adopted, which of course I wasn't; but my young mind couldn't understand why I was here on this planet.

It wasn't easy to grow up through all that.

Is that why you wrote that winning a

Grammar School Scholarship, at eleven years old, changed your life?
Yes. It raised me from the dullness around me and opened up a whole new world of finer thoughts. I can't explain the profound effect this had on me. Education made me feel like a fish at home in water, instead of gasping to survive on dry land.

Why did you write your books?
To share my experiences with others.

But why books, particularly?
Because they have a dogged determination to stay on people's shelves. They have a kind of permanence and they can be studied and read over and over again. I did my articles and tapes for the same reasons.

  I love books; they've helped me so much. They're priceless ways of reaching people. I've had thousands of letters saying how much my writings have helped others with their lives, so I think it's all been worthwhile.

Were they 'ghost-written', if you'll pardon the pun?
No, I wrote them myself — except for the public contributions, of course. From the beginning I had it contracted that the final

approval of the text would be mine, before going to print.

I felt that my voice, my message, shouldn't be watered down by third parties who might not understand my objectives.

In your books you say you found it difficult to cope with being renowned because of your quiet personality. Has that changed?
No. Either you like the limelight or you don't. I don't.

But media work generates public attention. Surely you knew that, and pursued it?
No. I've never sought personal publicity: I loathe it. They can cover my work and my message – I've had to get used to being interviewed – but as for myself, I just want to be left alone.

Are you concerned about the public 'living out' your teachings in their daily lives?
No, because that's their responsibility and not mine. I've never asked anyone to blindly accept any of my teachings. In fact, I've always said, 'Question everything.' How else can we develop our minds?

Can the future be seen?
Of course. Every soul carries its future

within it.

Can you see where orthodox religion is going?
Yes: downhill, and quite fast at present because it doesn't have the Living Power of the Spirit within it; and it'll continue to fall unless it's re-introduced.

Theology is sterile, just a set of barren words. Only the Power of the Spirit can breathe life into faith; and only true spiritual knowledge will satisfy the evolving minds of future generations.

What's your own religion, Stephen?
I've never 'labelled' myself, but I've been called many peculiar things!

Love and Service are important to me. Without the living expression of these, all religions are spiritually dead.

I value the right to think for myself and to be free to speak my mind, as well as to make my own spiritual quest.

My work is my work. Why do we need a label on it? I have worked for people of all Faiths and people of none.

In the British Spiritualist Movement I met people who helped me towards a greater realisation of self and the purpose of existence. But I've never belonged to any organisation as an affiliated member. I've always avoided signing membership books and adopting narrow views that might suppress my freedom of thought and spirit.

I work for the Great Spirit's Children and I belong to One Cause only — I belong to God.

Whom do you most admire, and why?
'Admire' isn't a word I often use, but I do respect people who are trying to be harmless towards others, the animal kingdom and the environment. And I've a high regard for anyone who, in the face of terrible adversity, can still be tolerant and loving.

Whom do you most dislike, and why?
Dictators and tyrants everywhere who dominate or damage others against their will.

What is your opinion of cryogenics: the freezing of human bodies, or heads, to be re-vitalised in the future?
It's a waste of time and money. Once the body's 'dead', the spirit departs.

Anyway, who would want to 'come back' sewn onto someone else's body? It's a dreadful thought. It would be an unspeakable genetic nightmare.

Why do you think you were born?
To evolve with and learn from others, as
well as to share with them many thoughts
and experiences.

In my opinion, we're all born with a soul
blueprint, but it's up to us to discover what
it is.

*What about your critics' opinions? Do they
bother you?*
No, but they trouble them.

*What about those who brand mediumship
'make-believe' or 'fraudulent'?*
What about them?

Do they unsettle you?
No, they can believe what they like.

*Does it concern you that your message hasn't
reached them?*
But it has. Why do you think they get so
frustrated?

No one can respond to the call of the spirit
until his or her soul is ready. Spiritual doors
stay firmly shut until they're ready to open.
That's the Law.

What are your thoughts about religious fanatics?
I think they'd be doing everyone a favour if they stayed in their churches and spent more time trying to develop the soul quality of toleration.

Religious fanatics haven't yet found themselves: they'll tell you that they have, quite loudly, but they haven't. What they've discovered is a cloak for their inadequacies, something which offers a false sense of security — and the clasps are made of fear.

What are your politics?
I have none.

But what about governments, aren't they needed?
Oh yes, I'm not an anarchist. Society needs fair structure. Without this, life would be quite miserable for many more people than it is now; but I don't think we've got it, do you?

How can politicians be respected when rich countries are burning huge amounts of excess food while poor countries are starving because they 'can't afford to buy it'?

That's a travesty of human rights, a sad example of the lack of spiritual advancement in the human animal.

I suppose politicians are trying their best, but many have forgotten that those who have too much should give to those who have too little.

I'd call that compassion.

Do you think there'll ever be a nuclear war?
Every weapon Man's ever invented has been used, and abused, by irresponsible hands.

I wrote a poem about politics and nuclear weapons:

Sunburst

The earth runs red with deep young blood,
  spilled by greed and avarice;
and the rivers boil with a crimson hue
  for the men who wanted more than you.

And the skies fade black
and the snow-storms come,
  as the daylight dims to twilight night:
    Someone burst the sunshine,
    to crown himself a King
    and subjugate with Might...

And a father's tears fall purple-red
on the lifeless corpse of his baby son;
    a bright light hurt him,
    maimed him,

```
        killed him:
        A finger-press — and the deed was done...

Only then did the Nations rise
against the men whose greed had run its course:

        but not before the death of millions;
        not before the children's cries;
        not before the holocaust...
```

*

Finally, if you die a wealthy man to whom will you leave your money?
(Laughing...) Pardon my mild hysterics at the thought of having plenty of money!

But, if it comes, I'd leave most of it to animal charities. People can work for their living but preventing cruelty to animals costs money; and so does the treatment of the unfortunate victims.

How would you like to be remembered?
I'm not bothered.

I expect some may remember me, but many won't; and I've lived long enough to know that no one's indispensable — absolutely no one.

What about your teachings?
Nothing is original; there are no new Divine

Revelations; they've all been given countless times before by others.

There aren't any new thoughts, just constant truths, re-designed to meet the needs of different generations.

The messenger is *not* more important than his message. The message will remain long after the messenger is gone; and that's the way it should be.

What about your own farewell, Stephen? What kind of ceremony would you like?
I don't want any fuss — just make sure I'm dead before you cremate me! (Burial is such a dirty business; if more people knew what happened to decaying bodies after they've been interred, they'd be horrified — they're so unhygienic, full of germs and diseases.)

At the service if someone wants to say a few words, don't let it be a clergyman or anybody who didn't personally know me — that would be hypocrisy. Perhaps my dearest friends might wish me well.

Make it a happy, musical occasion: play 'Going Home' as they carry me down the aisle and then sing some soul-stirring songs like 'You'll Never Walk Alone'.

Then, carry on with the great adventure of living.

And if someone sheds any tears, cry

because you loved me. Cry for joy, and not
for sorrow; because I'll be free — and Home
at last.

These Am I

I am a speaker of mysteries:
  but the pure in heart
    glean wisdom, hidden from the wise.

A toucher of souls am I:
  a shaker of death, to life.
    A lover of the loveless,
      can moisten tired eyes.
I believe the unbelievable:
  they make my spirit rise.

A stealer of time am I:
  so laugh with me
  and never die.

A Giver of Light I've tried to be:
  shining rays on darkened truths
  and revealing hidden lies.

I've never been a picture on a faded page,
  nor a smiling face
  without a mind to see:
    And you may know me,
    if you may know me...

12

Life Before Life

I was about to undergo another spiritual experience. It was a blustery winter's day and I was visiting an old neighbour by making the usual climb along a high path overlooking a steep grassy bank with trees dotted here and there, so I had to be careful where I was stepping.

The cold air caught in the back of my throat as I glanced down at my tired feet. Then — quite out of the blue — there came a vivid vision: instead of seeing my faded blue jeans and white trainers, my present-day clothes had vanished and in their place was a long brown monk's habit swinging in the breeze above bare sandalled feet. The vision was so real: I could even feel and hear the rustling of the thick cloth as it brushed against my legs and see long plaited cords that were dangling from my waist.

I blinked a few times, looked again, but the impressions had gone; yet they left sharp imprints in my mind on that frosty December day — and did so again whenever I experienced them on subsequent visits.

Deep inside I 'knew' I'd glimpsed my own past: the grassy bank and path had probably triggered some distant memory of a secluded region I'd lived in long ago as a Brother in a Silent Order (for I was keenly aware of absolute tranquillity while strolling along). And this made complete sense to me because I've always been happiest when wandering far away from the noisy world, at peace with myself; alone with my thoughts, alone with God.

Perhaps it sounds peculiar but my soul also knows what certain ways of dying *feel* like. I know what it's like to be shot: the impact, the numbing effect then the burning pain; I've been startled by the memory of my body hurtling downwards from a great height, my arms and legs flailing wildly as I neared the fast-approaching ground where I crashed to my death. I'm aware, too, of what it's like to be stabbed, garrotted, drowned — all these sensations are real memories because I think they could be connected to my previous lives.

Traumatic events linger in the memory-banks much longer than everyday occurrences. In my life as a monk, for example, I recall the rainy day when I slipped on the high muddy path and fell 300 feet below the monastery walls where my broken and bleeding body rolled into some thick bushes. My ribs were broken and one of my lungs was punctured. I was desperately ill but too far away from my Brothers to be heard. They believed me to be in my cell, fasting in prayerful seclusion; and hence they didn't find my body until a week later. It was in an unpleasant state of decay because I had 'died' on the morning of the third day, in dreadful agony and wracked with heaving pain...

I can't offer documented evidence of this spiritual memory for it took place far too long ago, but I can present my utter conviction that it happened. Some cynics might find this difficult to accept, but trying to measure spiritual experiences by material means rarely works.

The idea of living again on Earth is now becoming more and more widely held; hardly one of my public meetings passes without someone mentioning it. It's long been a deep-seated belief in Eastern countries, of course, but only a recent innovation in the West.

But is reincarnation a truth, a Universal Law?

Can we return to Earth as a completely different entity?

Have we been here before? And if so, what exactly happens to our individual survival after death?

And where are our loved ones who have already passed over? Are they still in the spirit world or have they been reborn?

Many are anxious for answers but, to my own mind, there'll always be room for heated debate and uncertainty simply because we're not all-knowing and can't possess every grain of absolute truth. The whole question remains perplexing because the cases for and against reincarnation are just as convincing, and in many instances are equally as strong as each other.

There's now such an immense wealth of evidence for rebirth scattered throughout the world, which suggests, at the very least, that it's probably a fact. And not all the recollections are glamorous, lurid or linked to famous royal families either; there are many folk who've claimed very ordinary pre-life memories when placed under hypnotic regression.

Extraordinary past-life experiences

certainly merit serious study and consideration, such as the incredibly detailed recollections of Joan Grant. Her 'Far Memory' series of books reveal her previous lives in great detail and they make riveting reading. In one of them, *Eyes Of Horus*, Joan recounts her days as a man — Ra-ab Hotep — the son of a high-ranking Egyptian official who lived approximately 3,500 years before the time of Jesus.

In this gripping life-story Joan recalls graphic stomach-churning details of how an elderly royal embalmer, named Yiahn, prepared a male corpse for mummification. It's an amazingly vivid description with such an incredible ring of authenticity attached to it that, as you scan the passage, you feel you're almost present, watching...

Joan writes of how the dead man's head was treated prior to embalming: the physician used 'a narrow strip of flexible metal' which was inserted in through the corpse's nose and then 'released... so that it held the nostril wide open'. Then the Embalmer grasped another instrument that had 'a handle the length of his palm, and at one end were two metal hooks curved like a leopard's claws. Up the nostril he thrust the claw; there was a grating sound like a mouse gnawing'.

She then watched him 'scraping the brain out through the nose: thick whitish curds flecked with blood and mucus; and carefully transferring them to the first of the jars'.

Powerful images, I think you'll agree, the details of which impressed Egyptologists who were studying possible methods of mummification.

In her fascinating autobiography, *Far Memory*, Joan Grant wrote: 'During the last twenty years, seven books of mine have been published as historical novels, which to me are biographies of previous lives I have known.'

Thought-provoking comments, but no more so than another extraordinary case of reincarnation concerning ancient Egypt, but this time stemming from the mind of Dorothy Eady who was born in Edwardian London in 1904. When she was three little Dorothy had an accident, falling head-over-heels down a flight of stairs. A doctor promptly pronounced her stone-dead.

But her family's grief changed into astonishment when they later entered the child's bedroom and found her sitting up in bed, having regained full consciousness. The doctor was amazed. 'But she was *dead*!' he exclaimed.

After this, young Dorothy began to have

strange recurring dreams, which later
turned out to be visions of ancient temple
monuments in Abydos in the Egypt of long
ago. She also perturbed her parents by
constantly declaring: 'I want to go home.'
Distraught, they couldn't make her
understand that she was home already, but
Dorothy would have none of it. Then
stranger things happened.

When they took her to visit the British
Museum the four-year-old girl further
perplexed her family by throwing herself at
the feet of the mummies, announcing with
fervour:

'Leave me! *These* are my people.'

As time passed, Dorothy began recalling
quite remarkable details of a former
existence as an Egyptian temple
priestess — named Bentreshyt — who was
also a secret lover of Pharaoh Sety the
First, about 3,200 years ago.

She said she had met 'His Majesty' (as she
always referred to him) and promptly fallen
in love with him in the spacious temple
gardens at Abydos, where — as the
fourteen-year-old Bentreshyt — she had
often walked amongst the flowers. Asked
where this unlikely mini-paradise was
situated she instantly replied, 'To the south
of Sety's Temple.'

The idea of luxurious trees and flowers in a desert setting seemed quite ridiculous to the experts, but they were soon to eat their own words. Surprised Egyptologists later *did* discover and then excavate this ancient Garden in the *exact* place where Dorothy Eady had located it. They even found an avenue of ancient tree-stumps and their deep root systems, plus a well and its irrigation channels for the lush green plants and flowers.

Impressive facts, indeed.

In adulthood as a citizen of Egypt, Dorothy took the now-famous name of Omm Sety; and as well as becoming a noted scholar of the ancient Egyptian religion and antiquities she also helped the authorities to translate many hieroglyphic writings, aided by her amazing far memories.

Up to her death she maintained an absolute conviction in an afterlife, even writing in her private diaries that the spirit of the 'dead' Pharaoh Sety regularly paid her night-visits in a fully materialised physical form.

Both Omm Sety and Joan Grant are well worth studying.

But before turning our full attention on the spirit people and hearing their opinions on reincarnation, first let's take a look at further evidence — offered this time by respected psychic artist Coral Polge who believes her mediumship has proven the existence of rebirth.

Coral is undoubtedly one of the world's best-known exponents of psychic portraiture. Her sketches of so-called 'dead' people (when compared to photographs of them taken in life) are quite startling, as featured in her book *Living Images* in which they are brilliantly verified by corresponding family snapshots. Coral's mediumship has been tested worldwide for decades. She's drawn pictures for total strangers from nearly every country you can think of, and several portraits seem to confirm that reincarnation takes place.

Here's Coral on Life Before Life:

As a psychic artist my work has been mainly concerned with the portrayal of people who have departed from their earthly bodies and are now returning to greet their loved ones still confined in this material existence.

But what of those souls who are now seeking to return to the Earth, not just in a portrait but in a new body?

Are they looking around for a suitable family to incarnate into, visualising what they may look like, planning a life-pattern to tackle?

A number of drawings have convinced me that souls do choose their future parents, and sometimes do so a long while ahead.

My first experience of drawing a before-life personality happened many years ago, but it was a considerable time before the recipient discovered what I had done. The picture was of a small boy with very large blue eyes and a quiff of reddish hair. Confident that he was part of her family, I was surprised to find that the picture meant nothing to my sitter and that no one in her family had red hair.

Many years later we met again and she told me the strange outcome to this story. At something like ten years after receiving the portrait, she was informed by a young spirit that he was coming to be her new baby; something she had no plans for at the time, her existing children all being in their teens and she in her late thirties. But he was already on the way, she discovered... And who did he turn out to be, but the little redhead I had drawn so long ago.

And here is another tale with an even stranger twist. A boy who had been miscarried came to be drawn for his father. I told the sitter that his wife had had two miscarriages, and that on both occasions it had been the same child trying to join their family.

'He will make it on the third attempt,' I explained.

The sitter didn't think his wife had lost a second child — but a few months later, she did.

Encouraged by my statement that he would eventually come into the earth world, they tried again, and this time all proved to be well.

But the nicest part of this story was the father's comment that they now loved him so much, knowing how hard he had tried to join them. 'It makes him so much more precious,' he said, when writing to tell me the outcome.

My pre-birth pictures convince me that we all choose our particular life, hard though it may be to understand.

Without doubt, these experiences raise deep and perplexing questions, as does this next snippet which also concerns a young spirit child but this time one who contacted his parents to correct their thoughts of reincarnation.

The youngster's message came through during a rare private appointment I gave to an anxious couple who'd lost their only boy through cancer. He was just a toddler, but he told his surprised mother who was now heavily pregnant again:

'I'm not coming back you know, Mum.'

Afterwards she explained:

'I thought this new child I'm carrying would turn out to be my deceased son, reincarnating as another boy.'

She then told me that she and her husband had been privately discussing this days before, but the bright-eyed spirit lad must have heard their ideas and arrived at the sitting to 'put them right'.

She later gave birth to a beautiful girl.

Staying with the theme of children for a moment, here's an intriguing story of a previous existence and how it strongly affected the subject's current lifetime, as told by a mature teacher named Val. It started in 1965 after she and her husband had walked up a spiral staircase in Pembroke Castle's Norman keep, in West Wales. Val went up the stairs easily, but at the top she was gripped by a sudden irrational fear:

I was heavily pregnant with my first child, but having always been fascinated by castles I enjoyed the climb up a spiral staircase in Pembroke. I'd been in many castles as a child, going up and down stairwells, and had

never had any bother at all, but on that day
I was very apprehensive and frightened.

My fears were all linked with *coming down*
the spiral staircase.

I know it sounds silly, but I couldn't help it.

But eventually I gathered my thoughts
together and, being practical, put it all down
to normal pregnancy fears and descended
carefully. After that, I thought no more
about it.

Ten years later, Val wasn't pregnant this
time but she was visiting another ancient
monument when a strikingly similar
experience befell her in an English city:

My husband and I had been sightseeing in
York, and of course the ancient Minster was
a must on our list of things to be seen.

We climbed the spiral staircase to the roof
of the south transept, over a hundred feet
from the ground, in order to have a good
view of the historic city. I had no problem
going up, in fact I never even gave our
ascent a second thought; but when we
turned to come down the narrow winding
stairway I was seized by an uncontrollable
fear.

I was petrified.

I didn't want to go down, but of course one
cannot stay for ever on a cathedral roof, so

the terror had to be faced even though I was momentarily 'paralysed'.

'Hold tightly to me,' encouraged my concerned husband, 'And we'll make it together.'

I felt so dreadful; my legs went like jelly. I was shivering and sweating profusely and my stomach was churning like mad, and I felt that all the blood had drained out of my body.

I couldn't move: I froze to the spot in terror, and it was only my husband's persistent and gentle persuasion that eventually led me down the staircase, very apprehensively. But even then, I was terrified, and I can remember the fear being so strong that I was scratching at the walls with my nails as I descended.

My husband said I was green-faced by the time I collapsed into a chair at the bottom. I was quaking all over, and fit for nothing.

Val desperately wanted to return to their hotel, where she flopped, exhausted, onto the bed:

My husband, seeing my unsettled emotional state, and being a hypnotherapist, suggested he should relax me and try to find the reason for this intense and sudden fear. I agreed, and an amazing tale spilled out of my mouth.

Under hypnosis I claimed I had lived in a Scottish castle, centuries ago. I had clear memories of being up a flight of spiral stone steps and gazing wistfully out of a very high window across to the horizon.

I then became aware I'd just got welcome word that my husband, in that lifetime, was returning home unexpectedly, so I excitedly ran down the spiral staircase to greet him. I was very pregnant and all of a sudden I tripped and fell heavily on the steps, tumbling right down to the bottom of the winding staircase.

I didn't remember any more.

Yet, oddly enough, as I was recalling this dramatic incident, during the hypnotic regression my current husband was simultaneously visualising and recollecting this entire scene: in his mind's eye he could 'see' it all.

He said I was attired in an elegant full-length gown and wearing a tall pointed wimple with a long, flowing white gossamer train. Furthermore, he realised my heavy pregnancy was six or seven months advanced.

Five years passed and Val was now leading a very active teaching career when she gradually realised that she was ill:

To my absolute amazement my doctor discovered I'd recently been pregnant and had suffered a miscarriage in its very early stages.

I was deeply shocked and disturbed, because I had no idea I'd been expecting a child, especially as I was then in my forties when pregnancies can be medically difficult.

Not only did the news of losing the very-early-stage foetus stun me, but it also completely drained me of energy. Although the doctor said I'd be back to normal in a fortnight, I just couldn't seem to get better. In fact I became so poorly and unwell that one night, while feeling terribly ill, a strange fear crept into my mind: an irrational fear which my intellect couldn't dismiss or explain away.

I was frightened enough to wake up my husband with some disturbing news, expressed earnestly.

'I feel dreadful,' I said. 'I feel as though I'm going to die.'

And then — I was immediately struck by a peculiar thought: this experience might be linked in some strange way with the pre-life memory of my miscarriage in the Scottish castle centuries ago when I'd fallen down the steps. So straightaway I asked my husband if he thought I'd died in that incident. Without hesitation he replied:

'You must have done, for you were six or seven months pregnant and it seems highly unlikely you'd have survived such a harrowing experience in that day and age.'

Then the strangest thing happened. As soon as I had linked these two similar events together — connected cross the centuries — *my fear of expecting to die completely disappeared* and was replaced by the realisation that, subconsciously, I'd thought I was going to die after this miscarriage because I'd done so before, in my previous life.

This incredible thought suddenly and instantly released my irrational fear of death.

Val now realises that once the key to a fear is truly discovered the owner can then unlock its cruel grip on the mind.

Psychologists share her views.

Now she's convinced that she really did live before as a pregnant woman, centuries ago in a Scottish castle:

I now believe that not only do we have many different lives, but also that any traumatic experiences we've undergone in past existences can, and sometimes do, trigger off similar effects in this life — right now.

What, then, can we make of all this?

Is reincarnation a fact?

People say that if anyone knows the truth it would surely be those advanced souls on the Other Side of life. Well, I wouldn't necessarily agree because it all depends on the mind you're questioning; even in the Beyond they're divided on this vital issue. Some claim it as an absolute truth, while others hotly deny it.

Older spirit guides usually state reincarnation is a Universal Law and it therefore does occur, but when you ask why other spirit people refute this, they reply:

'Many souls have not yet sufficiently evolved to appreciate its existence. Knowledge comes only to those who have unfolded their awareness to the point where they are ready to receive it; the right to know has to be earned.'

As for myself: I believe in God and that with God all things are possible. Not very scientific, I know, but then does everything have to be?

There are so many inexplicable mysteries in this vast universe of ours, how can we who are physically *finite*, fully comprehend the spiritually *infinite*?

We cannot, which is why all intelligent

people should keep an open mind.

So if reincarnation is a Law, *what* comes back? I don't believe *you* as a personality, a characterised soul, will return to Earth. But what *can* be reborn into flesh may be another aspect of your eternal mind.

There's a great difference between your Personality and your Spirit. The Personality is everything that you are in your physical consciousness — whereas the Spirit is the everlasting *essence* of you, the direct Life-Force which links you to God, the Great Spirit. So in your current form, as *this* particular physical individual, I don't believe you'll ever return to Earth, but you will pass on into eternity to live there for ever.

However, another portion of your Spirit, your Mind, might be characterised into flesh again as a different entity at some future time. This means that your separate individual survival is assured.

Concepts like these aren't easy to grasp, but perhaps we can be helped by likening the Spirit to a many faceted diamond, segments of which are personalised into Earth consciousness as physical individuals — each part having a life of its own, but all derived from the same Life-Force. In this way we have a centralised core of Mind — us — while at the same time there are fragments of the diamond shining in different Earth locations at one and the same time, each aspect adding its lustre to the centralised Mind.

Here's an easier picture: a bicycle wheel portrays your Centralised Mind as the hub of the wheel with all the spokes projecting outwards to join the continuous Circle of Time: each spoke is a separate Life which touches the time-stream at different points in Earth's history.

All are interlinked, and yet they seem to be 'separate'.

However, I don't think reincarnation can be successfully proved even though there's a vast array of startling evidence put forward, for there are many other possible explanations which can nullify facts concerning 'previous lives'.

Neither do I think rebirth is as common an occurrence as some people would have us believe. If it does happen, then the individual realises there are valuable lessons to be learned or special tasks to be accomplished on this planet and, because of free will, undertakes the incarnation itself.

I do not accept the popular idea that higher authorities make souls return. Either we have personal responsibility or we don't. I believe we do.

So what, then, could be the alternative explanations for these pre-birth memories? There are several possibilities:

1. A vivid imagination.
2. A 'secondary personality' belonging to the subject, which surfaces under hypnosis and claims to be a different individual.
3. An ancient spirit entity who links with the subject's mind and relays either through thought-transference or mediumship its past memories.
4. The subject could be tapping into what Carl Jung called the 'Collective Unconscious', referred to in the East as the 'Akashic Records'. (This is a kind of complete cosmic library of all thoughts, feelings and deeds which have been recorded in the ether since the beginning of time.)
5. Remote viewing, in which the subject mentally perceives the Past then dramatises it as a Living Present.
6. Out-of-the-body recollections or astral projection memories, during which the travelling spirit body sees places and people while the physical vehicle is fast asleep. Then, when the

subject is awake, he or she may later recognise these places and people again.

7. Genetic Memories. Some authorities claim that ancestral memories could be passed down with the genes of the body.

8. Cryptomnesia: this is the recalling of films, TV, and all reading matter and conversations that have been heard or seen when younger, which now surface as a dramatised 'life'.

9. Multiple Personality: a psychiatric condition in which it is claimed that one person can manifest several different personalities, with each one appearing at different times. It is also thought that each persona may be ignorant of the existence of the others, as well as of their actions.

Any one of these theories could broadly nullify rebirth memories, which is why I don't think the issue will ever escape doubt — though personal conviction is good enough proof for the perceiver.

But if we still doubt it, how could this last baffling case be explained away? It's one of the most fascinating stories in favour of reincarnation that I've ever heard, related by professional hypnotherapist Elizabeth Bowen, BA, Dip Ed, CC, CHP (College of Hypnotherapy and Psychotherapy).

The case came to her attention in the early 1980s and concerns a young healthy man in his twenties who was totally blind — and had been so since birth. As a newborn baby he'd been placed in an oxygen tent and too much gas was delivered, which caused the malady.

He approached Mrs Bowen because of 'unsettling dreams' he'd been experiencing which seemed to 'centre around the brilliance of the sun'.

When she regressed him, to her amazement he exclaimed: '*I can see!*' He went on to describe himself 'inside a wooden hut, in natural light, roughly carving the butts and handles of rifles so that the men could then later shape them to their individual shoulders and physiques for comfort'. His visions were in full colour and he could even see and describe in accurate detail 'the trees and the forest outside', objects which he had never seen before.

Quite a remarkable feat; but even more so when Elizabeth regressed him further back into what he could also 'see' was some kind of ancient tribe of which he was a member. They were worshipping the sun and had been instructed by the elders 'not to look upon the disc' as it rose. Being 'curious' in that lifetime, he disobeyed the law, was seized and then 'sacrificed on a stone altar'.

At the end of these incredible experiences, upon return to normality the young man was once again blind. 'It's one of the most interesting and baffling cases I've ever come across,' said Mrs Bowen.

I would certainly agree.

She ended by asking, 'How can this be explained, except that my client must have had some kind of previous existence in which his eyes functioned correctly?'

Finally, I'd never be forgiven if I didn't allow one of my spiritual teachers, my friend White Owl, to address this issue. But it's worth recording that while I keep a healthy open mind on many of these topics, he, it seems, is totally convinced of the existence of reincarnation.

Here's how he answered the question: *If there are previous lives before this one, why?*

Because the soul can only build its experiences through the crucible of learning.

Earth is a training-ground for souls; it presents unique opportunities to interact on a physical plane with many and varied other beings at differing levels of soul-growth to one's self.

In my world, the spirit plane, souls are naturally and automatically grouped together according to their evolution and growth. But in your world no such formal grouping takes place — your planes of thought are comprised of millions of beings all at different stages of evolution: all together; all interacting in one place; all growing through their challenges, struggles and experiences.

As a conscious being, first you are partially aware, a Divine Spark clothed in a beast; then you walk erect. Maybe you are poor, after which you are materially wealthy; sighted, then blind; ignorant, then intellectual; maimed and then whole; you are a male, then a female; lost and wandering — and then finally secure in your knowledge of self and God.

After this comes the greatest lesson of all when the soul learns to climb upwards towards the light, until it fully knows and expresses the true meaning of service, love and kindness...

You cannot learn all that Earth-life has to teach in one incarnation, for the Great Spirit has ordained that wisdom may only be possessed by the wise.

13

A Purpose to Living

Some of Life's Certainties

Do we now possess more wisdom because of our enquiries into the world of soul? Where have our investigations led us?

Amongst the turbulent sea of life's uncertainties and doubts: birth, life, death, life before birth, life after death — of what can we be sure? Well, I believe there are a number of points.

No soul is born without a purpose: we each possess a complicated spiritual blueprint which we bring with us into Earth-life. This deep soul-pattern may well have been built up through several incarnations, through many life-experiences – all of which add to the completeness of the whole individual.

Birth provides an excellent opportunity of returning to an existence where mankind and the animal kingdom are both thrown together in a miasma of confusion caused by the interaction of beings at all different stages of evolution. Here, each soul struggles to develop its innate qualities alongside others trying to do the same. And out of all this will eventually emerge further spiritual growth and order in the human race.

But while we exist within this seeming chaos, if we examine our lives carefully we can see that the broad outlines of our days are planned — by us; for we lead a double existence: twelve hours on Earth and twelve hours in the World of Spirit, where we truly belong. In our sleep-lives, older minds impart wise counsel to us (should we desire it) about what we were born to attain, about our past achievements, about where we are now, and — probably the most important guidance of all — about where our present thoughts will lead us.

So when next you wonder 'Where on Earth am I going?' try to remember:

Your Inner Self knows everything...

If you can learn how to touch your own Higher Mind (the elevated part of your consciousness which is not normally perceived without some effort) you'll discover through contemplation and prayer priceless inner guide-posts which will not fail you.

All the answers are within.

Even so, countless souls still remain pathetically lost and sadly wandering in the dark absence of knowledge, still painfully unaware that they've chosen their lives and could be at peace with themselves, if only they would seek it.

A young disabled man I know — he's wheelchair-bound — deeply searched his soul for many years, desperately trying to come to terms with his illness and the reasons for it. With all his might he valiantly fought his disabilities every inch of the way, until eventually he won his reward. It was a harsh but, paradoxically, benevolent dawning of realisation:

'Now I finally know,' he said with resignation, 'that I chose this unresponsive body because it has taught me lessons I never would have learned otherwise.'

Following this, a great well of peace was released within his spirit, the life-giving waters of which rose and bathed him in contentment. He immediately ceased to fight himself, saw the spiritual benefits of his misfortunes, accepted them gracefully, and now he's a much happier man. He even looks forward to waking in the morning, whereas previously he dreaded each new dawn.

Because of the increased tides of peace and power newly released within him, he realised a Constant Truth: *we can blame no one for our lives but ourselves*.

When others emotionally hurt us, we are to blame — it is our own fault, for we've allowed them to cause us harm. By opening ourselves to their poisonous arrows we have received them squarely in the heart (and sometimes all too willingly).

But in every life, suffering is inevitable. Earth-souls are constantly battling against one another, struggling to survive, to expand and mould the character. As human beings we're also for ever fighting our own selves, within. The beast of flesh seeks power over the spirit, and the soul endeavours to come into its own and thereby vanquish the enemy.

The eternal part of ourselves does everything in its power to master the physical temple and all its frequently selfish, narrow-minded thoughts.

We are engaged in ferocious mental and spiritual warfare within ourselves, a conflict which unbalances the harmony of the triune being that we truly are: body, mind and spirit. This war continually challenges the mind and builds up more soul experiences:

and thus we learn and slowly we evolve.

Life on Earth provides us with wonderful opportunities to develop ethically, morally, spiritually, physically, mentally and emotionally; and no one can escape these powerful life-shaping forces. All creatures will have their eyes filled with tears, their hearts wrenched with the pain of loss, and their minds confused by the trials of the spirit as it seeks to overcome its past and mould its future more fruitfully.

But thankfully, we shall also know compassion and taste the joy of spiritual and physical love; we shall smile and laugh and feel that life is indeed worthwhile when we are surrounded by those who love us.

Without exception, every soul must know the pleasures of success as well as the torments of adversity.

And as we travel forward, it's an absolute certainty that we won't always agree with our fellow-creatures, which is why our judgements should be guarded. Unless we've walked in the other man's shoes — intimately known and felt his every inner struggle, joy and personal despair — we cannot pass judgement on the quality or meaning of his life; though many believe they can, and therefore frequently do.

The act of condemning others is nothing

more than a simple psychological mind-trick: by casting suspicion away from ourselves and onto someone else, we hope that our own faults will avoid detection.

But in performing this action we lie to ourselves – and our time would be more wisely spent on examining our motives.

'Man know Thyself.'

This vitally important concept will help us to find our peace in this world. We can pray until kingdom comes to obtain 'a purpose to our days', 'happiness', 'our heart's desire', or any other 'possession' we'd like to 'own' — but none of these will ever be granted as a gift.

All soul-qualities must be earned. This is a Universal Law which cannot be abrogated or cheated: *Cause and Effect* decrees that we will receive *exactly* what we have earned for ourselves; we reap only what we've previously sown.

And during this eternal quest, every single scar or moment of joy is indelibly registered on the soul. Nothing is ever wasted or forgotten. The mind is a picture-making, recording substance: an Essence of Spirit Consciousness Itself which, when we think of something, images it as a reality. Rather like a 'living' movie our thoughts are projected onto the screen of our lives.

We are the originators: we create the plot, write the script, engage the other participants, direct the action, and also play out the drama ourselves.

And because each line of dialogue is for ever stored, filed away in a vast living memory-bank (an ever-accessible energy-pool or library of experiences) not one idea or expression is ever lost: they all remain 'alive', deep within the furthest reaches of the mind.

Nothing is ever 'finished', 'lost', 'irretrievable' or experienced without some 'hidden' purpose.

As we evolve, this experience-gathering mind of ours soon recognises that Life is full of comparison: light as well as shade. Who wants to live in a world where the blazing-hot sun never stops shining? I don't; I'd desperately miss the cool of the night. And how could we treasure the peaceful harmony of a healthy body unless we've first known the misery of pain? How could we truly appreciate the Earth's beauty from a high mountain peak unless we've first won the privilege of viewing it by scrambling up the steep and craggy hillsides, fingers bruised and aching as we grasped for hand-holds?

Only on the mountaintop can we know

that we've risen from dark and miserable valleys below, places that were once our homes before the powerful Light of Progress urged us forward.

But we must always seek, before we can find.

Life involves constant change, evolution; it is a journey of the soul from the darkness of mental slavery into the effulgent light of self-government and spiritual realisation. We can, however, make life's road much easier for ourselves.

By removing Negative Mental Forces and adopting Positive Thoughts we can welcome our challenges. When we're truly grateful for them, they cease to be our enemies and start to become treasured friends – allies that can teach us priceless spiritual lessons, both here and in eternity. (Life in the next world isn't easy, either, and progression is an everlasting process.)

Destructive Negative Forces thrive in grumbling statements such as 'Why did this terrible thing happen to *me*?' Or 'Why didn't someone else suffer this tragedy?' Or 'Look at others — they've lived privileged lives; nothing bad has ever happened to them'. All these are shallow-sighted lies, for the Sea of Life tosses everyone hither and thither in a turbulent mass of experience, no matter who we are, or who we might think we are.

Discontented souls are inexperienced beings who are out-of-touch with their higher selves, unaware of their true purpose and motivations. What these people are actually saying is: 'I don't want to mature; I don't want to evolve and change for the better — I want everything my own way.'

This is the hidden child speaking in us; an undeveloped being who wants the hardest tasks accomplished for him, without accepting any of the responsibility himself.

So many people make their own lives, and those of others connected to them, utterly miserable by carrying huge amounts of 'excess emotional baggage' within themselves. This usually takes the form of crippling negative emotions and energy-consuming worries, which they point-blankly refuse to drop.

Much physical illness is generated psychosomatically — by an overall negative attitude of mind. If we would just release these disharmonies, we could be free of all disease and subsequently achieve much happiness. There's a marvellous story which illustrates this:

Two saffron-robed monks were walking quietly along a riverbank, deep in silence and contemplation, when all of a sudden they came upon a distressed old woman who wanted to cross the stream but felt too frail and fearful to do so. The younger monk lifted her into his strong arms, carried her across the currents and deposited his grateful charge on the opposite bank. He then re-joined his colleague to continue their journey.

They walked on for a further mile or so in silence, but the older monk was inwardly boiling with anger because their religious order forbade any contact whatsoever with women and his younger colleague had flagrantly disobeyed this command.

After another mile the furious elder suddenly broke his vow of silence and severely and aggressively reprimanded his friend, to which the young monk calmly replied:

'Brother, I put that woman down two miles back: why are you still carrying her?'

Without doubt, the deeper problems of the soul are infinitely complex, so there are no easy answers, no instant solutions. This makes the path of soul attainment a long, slow and arduous one, with treasured prizes being garnered only one at a time, through struggle and personal effort. There are no short-cuts, there is just hard work and finally, the indescribable joy of self-discovery which brings a greater awareness of our own consciousness and how to control it, and with it — our lives.

We are personally responsible for our lives, actions, thoughts and deeds: no church, no book, no creed, no belief, no 'magical formulas' or divine beings can negate this Law. We cannot live utterly selfish lives and then upon death expect our actions to be wiped away and 'forgiven' by anyone except the souls to whom we have caused the suffering.

We ourselves will have to 'right' all the 'wrongs' we have committed.

We reap exactly what we have sown, every time.

This is Divine Justice.

We are the masters of ourselves, the captains of our own destinies; and there's nothing so insurmountable that it can obstruct or prevent us from steering the ships of our lives through peaceful waters, if that's what we really want.

And at the end of the journey, there is no such thing as death. Within us there is a spirit body through which we will continue to be conscious in a world of light nearby.

Progression — evolution — is open to every soul; and I believe the way forward is through expressing the powers of love and compassion.

And so the pageant of life continues.

The great adventure is a never-ending pilgrimage, a ceaseless struggle towards perfection.

Although I'm often categorised as 'a man in contact with another world', the implications of my work reach much deeper than this. Through all aspects of the written and spoken word and mass-media appearances there's been a far more important message underlying my voice than the fact that we survive death – and this is the conduct of the soul of man.

I've never been one bit concerned about the 'dead', for they're quite able to take care of themselves. It's the so-called 'living' who need our attention: the millions of people thronging the Earth who need encouragement to seek peace, tolerance, brotherhood, love and understanding; harmony, friendship, kindness and compassion; mutual respect for other life-forms and this small planet on which we must all dwell together.

Only by shining these qualities in our own lives can we ever hope to affect and change the lives of others for the better. These concepts are far more important to me than the fact that we cannot die.

What really matters is that Man learns to live at peace with himself and others.

It also matters that the animal kingdom should finally receive the love and respect it deserves; and that it shouldn't be exploited, tortured, maimed or 'scientifically' experimented upon by those who foolishly believe that progress comes by the shedding of innocent brotherly-blood.

My message is far from new; many seers and prophets down the ages have advocated it. But if only all the family of Earth, every race and nation, all sects and creeds, the rich and poor, believers and non-believers, would strive to light a lamp of understanding, brotherhood, love and peace within their hearts — what a wonderful world this could be.

The Wise Ones in the Spirit Realms consider it a privilege to serve, so much so that they've willingly renounced their places in exalted spheres to return and teach us more of these concepts. And why? — *Because they love us.*

Despite Man's constant foolish attempts to blot out their pristine Truths of the Spirit with unnecessary creeds, dogmas, ritual and priest-craft, some shining pearls of wisdom still remain, thank God.

Like countless voices before me I've asked mankind to stop, think, change – and spiritually progress. But at the end of the day, like everyone else, I'm simply a messenger whose message is far more important than its deliverer.

One day, when your life here is over, you will return to the realms from whence you came. Your finite body will crumble into dust — back into the heart of the Great Mother who gave it — but in the Next World your soul will rejoice in the knowledge that somewhere, somehow, your experiences, like mine, will have added something to the evolution of the human race.

In the next world, I guess I'll be grateful for the privilege of spreading knowledge of some of life's spiritual realities to people on Earth.

But what about you?

How will you view your time on this planet?

Only you will be able to answer.

But however you'll feel about it, the same rules will have governed us all: we will have realised there's no such thing as Chance, only *Cause and Effect*. We will realise that what we have sent out into the Great

Stream of Life is exactly what has returned to us, in full measure.

This vast Universe is ruled by a highly-organised Ancient Mind, of which we are each an integral part. We are the Eternal Sons and Daughters of the Living Light; Brothers and Sisters; gods-in-the-making, using the magnificent and inexhaustible Power of the Great Spirit's Thought and materialising it through our individual lives on Earth, and also in Spirit.

The Great Spirit is Indestructible and Everlasting — and so are we.

The Great Spirit

And in bewildering confusion, Man looked up and cried out from the depths of his Being: 'God, who art Thou?'
And as silent as a whisper upon the wind there came a mind-voice, speaking:

I Am all that Is.
  I Am in all things,
Through all things,
  Behind all things:
The Fire of Life
  Within a babe;
I shine behind your lover's eyes,
  A Power, crystallised.

278

I Am the Positive
And the Negative,
  Good and Bad;
  Love and Hate.
I Am black and white
  And a myriad shades of grey.
I Am in the rolling thunder
and the fire-fly's light;
  I Am the morning
  And the night;
The Darkness and the Light.

See me in soft gentility,
  And also in every cruel act:
For I Am Everywhere,
  In Everything;
  Within all life-forms
      no matter what they lack.

Neither male nor female I,
  But Spirit, Soul, Consciousness,
  A pulsing Breath of Life and Mind:
    The Beginning, which never was;
    The fleeting Now;
    And the very End –
      which man will never find.

Discover Me in a flowering bud
  Or glimpse Me in a looking-glass;
I Am the Unlovable;
  The Untouchable; The Intolerable –
In Everything which comes to pass.

The 'Is' Am I:
  A set of Laws,
  Laid down fast, Immutable,
  Unchangeable keys to all doors.
I Am discompassionately Sublime,
  Mathematically Perfect;
  I Am the Beater of Time.

And those attuned to Me,
  Harmoniously,
  Find peacefulness and ease;
But to those ignoring Me
    comes disharmony
    and dis-ease.

For I Am all Causes and their precise Effects:
  I Am inside the All
And outside the Everything you know;
  I fill the Nothing,
And yet I Am the Nothingness also.

And I need no worship or genuflection
Nor petty appeasements:
  For I Am not an 'I' —
  I simply Am all things:
And you are my reflection.

And unto you is granted
A measure of My Power,
  For use, according to your Willing;

For You and I are One —
And We are Mind,
Evolving.

PART TWO

Life in the Beyond
Glimpses into Eternity

Earth is but a Fleeting Dream,
Faint Shadows cast
by Greater Lights Beyond:

only the Essence
may know the Source;

only the Soul
maps out the Way;

and the Spirit is for ever
In Touch with Eternity...

14

Visits to the Astral Worlds

I

It was a quiet and peaceful summer's night, but I was far too tired to enjoy it. Although it was only four o'clock in the afternoon I felt quite exhausted, having been touring Britain taking public meetings for what seemed like centuries. I had to get my feet up on the bed and lie down, just to gather my energies.

When I closed my eyes, my legs felt as heavy as lead and my feet were throbbing. My cat laid down beside me, purring, as unconsciousness crept slowly through my mind and the blackness behind my eyes began to swirl with radiant glowing colours. Then, strangely, the rainbows suddenly swept aside and beyond them I could see some deep green grassy fields. Their vibrancy was marvellous, so enticing that I seemed to float right across into them, as if they were beckoning me. Only then did I realise that I was once more in touch with eternity, having crossed over to the Other Side of Life on another out-of-the-body excursion.

The blazing sunshine was beating down on flowering fields, blessing everything with great vigour and making it so alive and beautiful. For a moment I didn't want to walk on but just wanted to savour the radiant light and drink it in. So I rested under the shade of a large spreading tree, perfectly at peace and happy to be bathed by the living energies all around me.

I don't know how long I stayed in the cool shade; I may even have slept awhile: there are no clocks in the Beyond or sunsets to indicate the passing of time.

Refreshed, I rose lazily and decided to take a stroll, wandering across some fields and paths towards a building I had spied in the distance. At least, I'd thought it was a building until I approached it when the sunshine revealed it was a kind of natural amphi-theatre, formed from the gently sloping hills. Wanting to enter, I climbed a hillock and approached the powerful voice which I could hear lecturing within.

As I reached the top I could see from my position that the place was three-quarters full of all kinds of people. Elderly folk, the young and healthy, and whole families complete with boisterous children were all seated on natural grassy ridges which seemed to have been cut into the sides of the hill. All different races, creeds and colours were there; the common bond uniting everyone was the silence and undivided attention they were giving to an impressive speaker beneath them on the semi-circular stage.

Looking at the listening hundreds I became aware through my spirit body senses that these were mostly New Arrivals, people who had recently 'died'.

Then I thought, 'I recognise that deep voice,' and upon telescoping my sight I saw my spirit friend and teacher, White Owl.

I sat captivated by his eloquent speech and was eager to listen to his wisdom.

Like me, the crowds were enthralled by his common sense and gentle but powerful authority. Even though the amphi-theatre was vast, holding some 2,000 people, his calm voice carried effortlessly to every listener's ear. And as he spoke, his kind eyes took in all sections of the auditorium.

'Here, there is no time as you knew it on

Earth,' he said. 'Night is unknown because our atmosphere is so high that our sun's light cannot be hidden from us: it is radiated throughout our spheres and we have constant day, with sometimes short periods of twilight.'

'How can that be?' asked a long-haired youth near the front, who was resting his chin on drawn-up, clasped knees.

'Think of the polar-regions on Earth: there, day and night last about six months each because of the elevation of the sun. Here in our world there is a much higher atmosphere than that of the Earth and therefore our sun's rays are constantly glowing all around it.

'On Earth, after sunset, if your atmosphere extended much further out into space as ours does, you, too, would have no night. Your sun's luminescence would be bounced off the high atmosphere all around your globe, sometimes giving a kind of twilight; and that is what happens here.'

'Oh,' said the questioner, pondering on the lesson. 'When do we sleep then?'

White Owl continued: 'I have been here for many centuries, as you think of time, and rarely have I needed sleep, though I have occasionally rested near streams and often in the company of good and faithful friends.

Sometimes I have changed my surroundings to rid my mind of old habit-patterns and travelled out into the deeper realms of the Spirit World to visit the Shining Ones and the Masters, from whom I obtain great soul-strength and an inexpressible peace of mind.'

The crowd listened intently as I observed that his auric and mental fields were sensing their immediate needs. My psychic exercise completed, he addressed them again:

'So each of my "days", as you understand the term, has no beginning and no end, for we exist here in the Eternal Now.

'There is much to occupy us, great service to perform. When I am not taking counsel with older minds I might be called to any point in the World of Spirit or on the Earth, where help is needed.'

'How?' asked the inquisitive student again, and, even though he was interrupting, the crowd didn't seem to mind; there were no grumblings. I sensed intuitively that they had already learned patience. In Eternity there's plenty of time to sit and listen. What's the rush when you have for ever stretching out before you?

'We speak by Thought,' answered White Owl, resplendent in his purple and lilac spirit robes, which reached from his broad shoulders down to the pearl-coloured platform. 'Thought and Mind are the Powers that link all beings together, in whichever plane of life they exist.'

It was then that his deep brown eyes engaged mine at the top of the hill (though I've no doubt he knew of my arrival long before this) and with a smile flickering across his lips he incorporated me into his talk.

'Sometimes, the man who acts as my medium, of whom I was speaking earlier, sends me an urgent SOS call simply by Thought. It arrives as a small explosion of energy and acts like an alarm call within my mind.'

Then he demonstrated it, as all at once a brilliant blue-gold light — like a sudden flash of electricity — burst into being about three feet above his head. This impressed the crowd and sent a thrill of excitement buzzing through it.

'After receiving it I am able to retrace its path and home in on my medium's mind-frequency; and in an instant I can be beside him. Rather like physical Man, who has perfected missiles which follow a directional laser beam, in the same way I can find my medium.

'By *thinking* of our destination, Thought carries us there instantaneously, once we have learned to hold and project the images correctly. Although this sounds easy, in reality it requires much practice before it becomes second nature. But I can also tune-in, hear and see what is transpiring at any call's source without actually travelling there in my spirit body.'

The crowd began whispering, obviously intrigued by this latest remark, which again prompted the youth to ask:

'Is that what happens when we think we can sense an invisible person in the room?'

'Yes, indeed. But instead of our presence, you may simply be registering our thought-rays. It all depends upon your sensitivity at the time of transmission.'

There were lively exchanges amongst the hundreds while they discussed similar experiences. And when silence returned, a middle-aged nurse, who I sensed had only passed over recently, raised a question.

'Please, what happens when someone "dies"? I nursed many dear souls and tended to their sick bodies — but what about the spirit's release? Are special calls sent out then?'

He smiled at the woman and answered her as a loving father might address his child.

291

'At the points of passing, had your psychic vision been operating you would have seen many spirit helpers surrounding the travellers' beds. No one dies alone. Calls go out in the form of prayers or even just desires; and we are in attendance long before the transition occurs.'

'Thank you,' she replied, thoughtfully.

'And would you like to continue nursing?'

'Oh yes... yes, I would,' she said, thoroughly warmed by the secret he'd read from her mind.

'Then you shall, for there are many aspects of spiritual healing to be learned here. You may be one of the Watchers around beds of illness, if you so desire it.'

'Oh, I do,' she smiled. 'I'd like that very much.'

'Then so be it. Thoughts are reality here, and presently someone will come and help you to actualise them.'

Joy beamed from her face.

'Thank you. Thank you so much, my friend.'

'Ah...' he smiled. 'friendship! I have many great friends in several worlds; and it is now my privilege to count you as one of them. To be in the company of good friends is a wonderful experience: it renews the spirit, refreshes the mind and brings strength to step forward and serve. Life here is all about service, rendering knowledge and comfort to people existing in many and varied levels of being. Though never easy, it is a joy to aid those who are struggling for light.

'I have always been helped in my times of need and now I am repaying these debts. You, too, will render service to others. I know you will.'

'I shall,' smiled the nurse; and the crowd picked up these powerful emotions, vocally agreeing with her.

'To serve is a privilege. This is what attracts me here and also to my medium on Earth. He and I attune to each other because of the love and friendship we have fostered during our association.'

Then, as his compassionate gaze took in each face among the hundreds, he quietly outstretched his arms, which took with them the many folds of his glimmering purple raiments. With an open face and utter sincerity he whispered — and yet it was loud enough to be heard by all — 'Know that I am your friend, and you are all mine. And whenever you may need me, just call upon my name and I will answer.'

My spine tingled as I felt the great wave of love washing out towards him from the people; they were overjoyed to be in his presence and I felt proud to know him so well.

That was when I realised I'd been 'brought' here to see these aspects of his work.

Then an eight-year-old black girl, wearing a red-and-white checked frock, shouted from her place enthusiastically.

'Where's God? I haven't seen Him yet!'

After amusement had rippled through the crowd and then subsided, White Owl leaned forward and swept her up in his arms as though she weighed nothing at all. Self-consciously, she wound a finger around a lock of her hair and he smiled at her:

'I have been here such a long time and I have never yet seen a person who might be called God. And no one else here has, either. But I can see the love in your mother's eyes, there in the front row. Can you?'

The youngster put her finger in her mouth and nodded 'yes'.

'Well then, when I look into your mother's eyes I think I can see God shining out of them,' he said.

And with that she wriggled free of his grip and quickly ran to her mother's embrace, as he turned and informed the people.

'All we can experience are the many

manifestations of God, the many faces and forms of a Great Power, which appear on all levels of being both seen and unseen. A long time ago when I was incarnated on Earth, I belonged to the race now known as the Native American Indians. We lived close to Nature and worshipped The Great White Spirit.

'I still hold this concept: God as a Breath of Conscious Life. I can see no better way of expressing in human terms the Infinite Mind behind all Creation, a Supreme Mind which rules through Perfect Natural Laws.'

'But why can't I *see* Him?' the child persisted loudly. 'I'm not an Indian – I'm from Jamaica, and so's my mother!'

'Little one,' he smiled, as the audience laughed, 'you will come to know Him, in time. This I promise you.'

'Words,' he said to the crowd, 'are always inadequate when trying to describe Infinite Thought. Man in physical form is a Finite being; but God the Great Spirit is Infinite, spanning all eternity and incorporating universes and galaxies known to us, and others as yet undiscovered. God is a Power.'

'You mean like sunshine and electricity?' said the child, much to the crowd's delight.

'Yes,' he smiled.

But undeterred, she wanted to know:

'Well, where does He *live* then?!'

'Everywhere.'

Then through various archways, brightly-dressed spirit people entered, sought out and sat next to each group of listeners in the auditorium. White Owl seemed very pleased they'd arrived, no doubt at his mental beckoning. (In fact, I wondered if his earlier demonstration of how a spirit call is sent and received was actually a transmission asking these guides to collect their new arrivals?)

'Our visitors will now escort you to your people or to rest homes, or to wherever you might be happiest at present. Trust them and be happy. And the love of the Great Spirit be with you all, my friends.'

He raised up both his arms and there was instant applause from the crowd. I suppose it was a natural reaction, one of thunderous gratitude as he slowly faded from our sight in a vaporous mist, followed by a silent explosion of bright silver light.

I watched the joyous listeners leaving with their helpers, then I walked over the top of the hill, there to be greeted by White Owl who was awaiting me.

But I can't recall what happened after that; there's a blackness in my memory...

II

...Recollection returns as we were walking down through the lovely fields I'd seen at the start of my journey. White Owl was talking.

'Evolved minds can see people and events in different time-zones in the past, present and future – and also in different spheres – without the need to travel there. Like radio sets, they can pick up signals being transmitted thousands of miles away.'

'You mentioned many spirit spheres earlier. How many are there?'

'Some on Earth teach that there are seven, but I disagree. There are seven planes of thought near to your planet from which many souls communicate, but beyond these there are multitudinous worlds waiting to be discerned. Each time we think we have reached peaks in our evolution, there are further mountains ahead of us.'

'So there are countless worlds of spirit?'

'Indeed, and I have visited many of them because I'm quite an old soul. My stage of evolution enables me to travel way up into the higher realms as well as down to the Earth.'

His eyes were clear and full as he gazed across the beautiful fields rolling out around us.

'These scenes bring me great delight. We are quite close to Mother Earth now, but this beauty is as nothing when compared to my true home in the higher realms. It is difficult for me to express its wonder.

'After centuries of soul progression, upwards and inwards towards Perfection and the Light of God, outward shape and form becomes unnecessary.'

'You mean the Wise Ones have no bodies?'

'Individuality is retained along with character and soul experiences, but there is no need for any vehicle of expression other than pure Mind.'

'But how do they recognise one another there?'

'Awareness: a soul-knowing. Sight and sound are clumsy tools which are unnecessary there.'

'Have we many bodies before we lose our outward form?'

'Legion; after which individuality exists only as a focal point, like a distant star on a dark night.'

We were now nearing another location, a sort of open-air hospital or rest-place. I could see colourful beds and couches lying out in the sunshine in a kind of grove that was surrounded by flowering trees and cool shaded areas. My spirit body instantly registered the deep serenity and healing energies that surrounded everything.

'See! Our destination,' said my teacher as we reached the place.

'Are these people newcomers, too?'

'You have sensed it well.'

And we stood apart at a short distance and observed young spirit women and men in bright robes moving amongst the 'patients' who were sleeping on the couches.

'Many who are helped to make the crossing are surprised that they still exist.'

'I suppose few give serious thought to the possibility of an after-world.'

'Ah, but now they *have* to accept it. There is usually great laughter and many tears shed when their loved ones come to greet them. Watch now, and see.' And he turned me towards a shaded grove. 'There: the old woman is waking and her children are around the bed. Let us observe.'

And the elderly, refined-looking woman opened her eyes, stretched her arms up high and yawned away 'the sleep of death'. She rubbed her eyes in amazement at the sight of the four people around her couch. Her incredulous tone matched her expression.

'Arthur? Mavis?... Joe? Is that you? My

babies? But...' she sat up and leaned forward, '... but, you're all dead.'

'We never died, Mamma,' said Mavis, 'we simply went ahead and waited to greet you again, like this.'

'What...? You mean...? What...? I've...' And for a moment the educated woman couldn't summon the courage to speak the word. 'Have I... died?'

Three of her children smiled, except the fourth who was a tall young man sporting a thick mane of raven-black hair with silver-blue sunlight playing on it. He looked hesitant; and then his seriousness broke into a wreath of smiles as he stepped towards her bed.

'And who is this young man?'

There was an awkward pause, during which the stranger leaned forward and gently caressed and kissed his mother's face. Something inexplicable must have invisibly transferred itself to the old woman's soul when his lips met her aged skin.

'Oh...' she gasped, as realisation began to light up her features. 'Oh... Sebastian? Is it *you*, my darling? Oh... is it really you; my baby boy?'

'Yes, mother; it is me. All these years of waiting, but now we are together...' he smiled.

'Oh, my baby. My little boy...' she said, too overcome to say any more. And she threw her arms up around his neck and embraced him ecstatically while tears rolled down her cheeks. Then she found her voice again.

'How I wished you could have lived, my son,' she said. And I sensed her remembering that he'd only taken a few precious breaths on Mother Earth before he had 'died'. 'But how you've grown!'

The kind woman's face lit up with smiles as she embraced her once stillborn child, now a full-grown man, over and over again.

'Yes, I remember now, my son — I've seen you before, many many times throughout the years, in my dreams... It's all coming back to me now...'

'That's right,' he replied, brimming with joy. 'Every loving memory we've ever shared in your sleep-life will soon return to you, Mamma. Nothing will be forgotten. You're safe now, Mamma; out of your pain, and we're all back together again as a family.'

I can't describe the look of pure wonder on the woman's face as she clasped him tightly to herself once more and said from the depths of her spirit:

'Oh my precious, precious boy. Sebastian, my son... There surely must be a God, to have given you back to me.'

And her three remaining devoted children stepped back and cried at their mother's joy in Sebastian's arms. She could no longer contain her love for him, and her tears fell like rain on the shoulders of her firstborn. 'There is a God,' she whispered gently. 'There is a God...'

Both White Owl and I felt we were encroaching on a sacred moment, so in unison we moved quietly away to another corner of the gardens, where an old man had just become conscious...

III

'Come and speak with him,' said White Owl as we approached the golden couch the old gentleman was laying upon. He greeted us with a wrinkled, smiling face.

'Hello, my friend,' said the old man, 'I didn't think to see you again so soon.'

'Well,' returned my guide, 'God knows best when to call a traveller home.'

'Oh, I'm so glad to be out of my pain: the tears I've shed; the agony was unbearable, so terrible and great.'

'Yes, but it's all over now.'

And the two friends clasped hands tightly.

'Yes, I don't feel a thing any more, except

tranquillity. That big ball of pain inside my stomach has completely gone. It's been deflated!' joked the elderly arrival. And the three of us laughed together.

'This is someone I have known for many years on Earth,' said White Owl, indicating me at his side.

The old man lifted a gnarled and bony hand to vigorously shake mine. 'I'm very pleased to meet you, young man. Any friend of my companion is also a friend of mine.'

My teacher spoke again:

'Last time we met, when you were physically unconscious and we talked, you asked about the Judgement Day. Do you remember?'

'I do.'

'Well, now it has come.'

My teacher sat on a form beside the bed, motioning me to join him, which I did. But I wasn't intending to speak; I was content to just sit quietly and listen to these two friends. And I watched as White Owl took the old man's wrinkled hand and gently explained about the Judgement Day.

'You have nothing to fear, for there *is* none. When a soul passes, the spirit is freed and the mind dislocates from the brain to express itself through the etheric body. Then a number of memories are often seen

303

by the person "dying".'

'It happened to me,' said the enthralled traveller.

'Yes: it's said that a drowning man experiences this, too; and in a sense he does, though it is impossible to view an entire life in one second.'

'As I breathed my last, I saw a panorama of some of the more important parts of my life, pictures swirling in my mind.'

'Judgement happens over a long period as a soul slowly re-adjusts to its new life. This world is not strange to new arrivals, for they have passed in and out of it every night during sleep... like Stephen, here. He is not "dead".'

I smiled at the man.

'The higher self is well accustomed to the World of Spirit so there is no shock on passing. Is that not so?'

'Why, yes,' said the traveller. 'I feel that I belong here, my friend. Almost... almost as if Earth was now just a short journey away from this place. *This* is my real home now... like it used to be in my dreams.'

'That is so.'

'These astral planes are very similar to Earth, anyway,' I chipped in.

'Yes,' added White Owl, 'because they are populated by folk who have just come from there and they have created this environment by Thought.' He faced the old man again. 'You are very lucky, my friend, for you have knowledge. The saddest cases of all are those who have held no belief in anything. They find themselves existing but sometimes unable to fully comprehend that *this* is their reality now, and not some hazy dream.

'Think for a moment of the many times you have dreamed vivid dreams and recalled them. But what if you were never to wake up? The dream would be your reality, would it not?'

'Yes,' said the man, as though some brilliant light lit up his mind for the first time. His face was full of eagerness and wonder and he propped himself up on his forearms and inclined his head forward, listening intently as my guide went on:

'Adjustments must be made, of course, because you will eventually meet a number of people you may have wronged as well as those whom you dearly loved. So we constantly judge ourselves. Only through a process of purging the mind may we find peace within ourselves, by eventually reviewing and weighing all past acts, thoughts, words and deeds.'

'Tell me, dear friend, what happens next

to me, now?' asked the man.

'Oh, you can do as you please,' smiled my guide. 'There is free will here and no one will tell you what you may or may not do. There are arts, sciences, healing and education — many activities indeed. The choice is yours, unless you require guidance.'

'So I may please myself?' he asked, incredulously.

'Of course. But if you attempt activities beyond your current level of soul-growth or understanding, you will fail to execute them successfully.'

'Do you mean we must comply with The Great Spirit's Laws we talked of, some time back?'

'I do. They operate automatically all the time and we must all work under their giant umbrella and within the scope of their limitations.'

'I see.'

'However, help is always at hand if you need it. But then, hopefully you will learn from your mistakes.'

'How I value your help and friendship,' said the man with shining eyes, as he tightly clasped White Owl's hand. I simply watched and said nothing, content to witness this interchange of thoughts.

'And tell me, White Owl, for how long must I be old and crabbed like this, my dear friend?'

'Until you decide to change your appearance. Your spirit body is young and at the height of its strength and beauty, should you desire it. It is only your old thought-patterns that keep you aged.'

'I see,' said the man.

'Concentrate,' returned White Owl.

'I'll try...' And closing his eyes tight-shut he began thinking of himself as a much younger being, at the prime of life when he was a carefree youth; when he was fit, well and happy.

And as he did so, very slowly I watched a remarkable change overcome his form. Superimposing itself over the old shell there appeared a much younger image. He was transforming his appearance – by Thought.

And before long the wizened body had gradually dissolved and given way to that of a handsome man in his early twenties.

Now healthy and strong, he let out a sudden whoop of laughter and hopped out of bed like an athlete.

'Thank you, my friend — *thank you!*' he cried, dancing about on nimble feet and shaking our hands profusely. He was incredibly happy! 'But I mustn't waste another second. No more time! I must go now and find my people. I shall run!' he shouted, dashing towards the fields like a newborn pony kicking its legs with the sheer joy of being alive.

'Yes. Go and be happy!' cried out White Owl.

'Good luck!' I added, loudly, as the light-footed youngster skipped through bright carpets of flowers.

Nearby, the spirit helpers smiled and didn't bat an eyelid, fully understanding his sudden enthusiastic departure, obviously having seen it all many times before.

I then felt rather sleepy... or was my vision functioning incorrectly?

What was happening?

Maybe there was some kind of strange magnetic pull from my physical body back on Earth because suddenly the whole scene was disappearing in a swish of wispy white smoke — and I awoke back in my bed, twisting awkwardly in the night.

IV

I gained consciousness in the next world right in the middle of a conversation with White Owl.

'Some say animals have no souls,' he said.

'These people are misguided, for even the wildest animal has an etheric body within its physical form. Wildebeest, mice, leopards, tigers, elephants, all creatures have this energy body. Like other life-forms their physical bodies only hold together because they are built around the blueprint of the spirit body.

'All creatures have consciousness and personality albeit, in some cases, of a somewhat less advanced order than that of man. It is the Divine Spark of the God-Force within them which assures their survival.

'These souls have their own worlds but, of course, some creatures have lived with man for so long that through conscious co-operation, love and loyalty they have been helped into a greater awareness of themselves; and therefore have been aided further along the road of progress. Come; take my arm and I will show you.'

I obeyed – and the whole scene of greenery vanished and we found ourselves in a dark and dank-looking place. I didn't like the coldness which permeated the atmosphere there.

'This is the realm wherein dwell those who have showed dreadful cruelty to animals and human beings.'

'Where are the people?' I asked, noticing no signs of life anywhere.

'Hiding in those caves,' and he pointed them out nearby. 'They shrink from their shame, full of regret and the constantly-present memory of the cruelty and pain they inflicted on their brethren: it plagues their minds and disturbs the deepest peace of their spirits.'

I glanced around and spied several dark caves hewn out of the sheer cliff-face where we had arrived, and near which we were now standing. We were perched precariously on a small rock-shelf. I wanted to go inside a cave and talk to one of the people and my thoughts were instantly registered:

'I will take you nearer, but the rest is up to you.'

And in a twinkling of an eye we were immediately transported up onto a higher ledge in the cliff. I was balanced on a tiny ridge, just big enough for my two feet to creep along, provided that I kept my back to the slimy sheer rocks and my arms outstretched, in case I should fall.

Slowly, carefully, I edged my way towards a dark opening, my head pulled right back so that I could view only the strange sky. I was terrified to look down at the 400-foot drop into seeming black nothingness, way down below my feet. I never did like heights.

White Owl stood apart on a larger piece of jutting rock nearby, watching while I gained a surer footing and thankfully slipped inside the cave, into the thick blackness — where I saw no one at all. Neither could I, at first, hear anything except the steady dripping of water.

But I 'knew' there was someone in there.

'Hello? Hello there? I've come to talk with you. Will you show yourself?'

When the echo of my voice faded, there was silence — but strangely I sensed that somewhere in the shadows there was a huddled shivering figure of a sad and wretched man. Although he never made a sound, I strangely 'heard' his troubled thoughts but couldn't make out their confusion.

'Hello?'

'*Go away!*'

The sharp sound slapped me in the face and straightened my spine as if a sniper's bullet had been shot into it.

I recovered and tried again.

'Please, I'd like to help you if I can... Won't you step forward and talk with me? I won't hurt you, my friend.'

There was a further long silence... and no response.

So I stepped deeper into the dank rocky cave, gradually focusing my eyes until they spied the shaking form of a pathetically thin man. He was more afraid of me than I was of him; and as soon as he felt my piercing gaze he cowered back as far as the rocks would allow. He seemed petrified of my presence. His eyes widened and he drew his whitened fingers into a knotted fist, closer underneath his chin.

'I won't hurt you,' I said, quietly. 'I just want to help you, if I can.'

Silence again as he curled into a tighter ball of fear. It was then that I sensed the terrible sadness all about him. In a flash of a second I knew he was truly sorry for his past cruelty. I also knew what he had done: he'd been responsible for mutilating several horses and other animals, for 'sport' and 'pleasure'; but his tears were now shed out of regret.

'There's a much better place for you to live in,' I said. 'If you would only accept that you're ready to quit this dreadful place, I can help you to leave.'

'But I... I don't deserve to live with ordinary folk. What I did... what I've done is too cruel to describe... I am, so ashamed...'

'I know,' and by now my reassuring hand was resting on his sharp shoulder blades. 'I know everything that you did, but that's all behind you now. You can make amends for it somehow. You can't stay here for ever. It's time to move on. The time's right for progress and I've been brought here to take you onwards.'

And the huddled figure began to sob unashamedly. He clasped my legs and buried his head into them. When I bent down and touched his shivering form I noticed he could only have been about thirty years old, and his dirty shirt and trousers were covered in dried-up blood-stains: indelible impressions of heinous crimes, perpetuated by a horrified mind.

'Come along, now. Follow me, for you've suffered enough. Your memories have plagued you for far too long.' And I gently helped him to his feet, until he was looking right into my eyes. 'I've been sent to place you in the care of others nearby, and — if you'll just say the word — a much better life starts from now. And all you have to do is desire it.'

'I do,' he wept, his shoulders rising and falling under the powerful emotions rising in his breast. 'I do... But... it can't be this easy... not after all the harm I've done...?'

'But it is,' I assured. 'We can walk away together, now, or if you wish I can help you to sleep. When you wake up you'll be in a much better place. You've earned the right, you see. Just trust me, my friend. Your remorse is spent and these tears prove you're ready to make amends.'

'I am,' he whispered emotionally, his eyes brimming with new hope. 'Yes, I truly am, really – and I'll help the animals in any way I can now; I owe them this... And I do so want to rest.'

At this point, a smiling, kindly White Owl walked towards us, outstretching a hand which touched the man's brow — instantly causing him to fall asleep, as if some powerful anaesthetic had been miraculously delivered. And then the cave vanished.

White Owl and I stood together once more in the flowering gardens and the same young man was now resting before us on a prepared green couch. He was unconscious, his chest heaving like that of a tired child overcome by some deep and profound sleep. Three nurses and several helpers attended his healing bed: they were already transmitting energy-rays to him and were patiently awaiting his return to consciousness, health and balance.

'Will he ask for me when he wakes?' I said.

'No. But he will never forget you. All he needs now is rest. We can help him again later; and this time perhaps you would like to explain the Judgement Day. Would you?'

'Yes.'

'Good,' he said — and my memory faded out...

V

...Awareness returned within a dreadful atmosphere of utter confusion and fear, and the sickening vibrations so filled my mind that I panicked. Fortunately, I was next to my spirit guide who calmed me by his thoughts while I realised where we were. It was a place where animals — mostly cows, pigs, chickens and sheep — were suddenly 'appearing' on concrete-type floors of what could have been some kind of farm out-houses.

The animals seemed stunned, or looked as though they'd just collapsed of exhaustion. Many of them were rolling from side to side with their legs curled up tightly towards their bodies until they suddenly 'awoke'. They tried to scramble to their feet, terror-stricken in many instances.

The surrounding air was somewhat darker than in the other places we'd visited, and I instantly knew this atmosphere had been created as a direct result of the fear in the animals' minds. White Owl broke my sorrowful thoughts and spoke softly.

'We are in one of the many places where animals cross over after being slaughtered for meat, on Earth.'

My instincts had served me well, for I'd felt this was the case before I'd heard his voice.

'Are they just arriving?'

'Yes. Shocked and dismayed; stunned, as you can see.'

And I could. And as I took in the dismal surroundings, in one corner of the yard a cow 'appeared'. She was rolling on her stomach, on the ground, her legs seemingly quite useless as she lowed loudly. Then an kindly teenage girl — a spirit helper — dashed towards her and started to stroke her body and soothe her distress with gentle, comforting words.

'These good souls are kept for ever busy here, as you can no doubt imagine.'

I felt so sad that I thought my heart was going to burst. I was deeply troubled in the spirit.

'Do these poor creatures remain here long?'

'No. This is just the place of their

transition. They "died" at the merciless hands of man in his abattoirs. We bring them immediately to these similar man-made buildings. All their lives were spent in similar surroundings and arriving here considerably lessens the shock they receive. They will shortly be taken away to brighter spheres.'

'Animals have their own planes of thought?'

'Oh yes, except for the very domesticated ones like cats, dogs and other pets of all varieties; these stay with their human friends or with members of the family who have passed to this side. Wild creatures have their own spheres of activity.'

'And what will happen to this herd of cows?' I asked mournfully, pointing out into the courtyard where a few youngsters were leading several sad-looking animals further away from the out-houses and into lanes hedged with leafy trees.

'They go with these friends and then into their own worlds. There they will be left to find their own way of living.'

'What about farm animals who've grown attached to their owners and their children?'

'They remain with them, in fields and paddocks provided by the humans. Love is the Link. Only Love can build true friendship between any life-forms.'

'And the wild animals: is their continued survival assured?'

'Yes, if they desire it. Once consciousness is personalised into physical form it gains an individual awareness of itself — so survival is assured.'

'You seem to imply that some don't have continuous survival.'

'That is so. It all depends upon the level of Mind which the creature has attained in its struggle to progress towards a depth of awareness.

'As far as the animal kingdom is concerned, there is what we term the Group-Soul; and its influence is especially strong in their lives. In their own spheres, individual animals lose their identity into the amassed consciousness of the whole of the herd — if they so choose.'

'But doesn't that contradict the Law?'

'I can only reveal how matters are; I did not invent the Natural Laws. I am merely an observer, like yourself...'

VI

I'd tried to doze off in the armchair but had woken up to hear the rain sleeting against the windowpane. As I rose to close the curtains, I noticed how dark and bleak a day it was outside.

For a moment I stood and watched the sheets of hypnotic rain washing in at forty-five degree angles to the ground, sweeping in torrents down the deserted roads.

Sundays were always quiet when it was wet.

I wearily pulled the drapes on the grey deluge, turned up the gas fire and took up residence on my soft and comfy sofa, cuddling three pillows around my head like long lost friends.

Everything was so peaceful, warm and snug: my cat, Sooty, was curled up on the hearth rug and purring contentedly; and the inky blackness behind my eyes was velvety soft and marvellously inviting...

...My first memory was of a happy group of children seated under the shady branches of a large and spreading oak tree. I was standing just outside their circle; but alone, my guide was absent.

I felt I'd been there with him for quite some time, but now he'd left to attend to other pressing work while I observed this playful class.

The tutor was a slim man in his twenties;

and he wasn't an ancient soul — no, he was as young as his age and, I thought to myself, a relatively New Arrival to the Spirit Side. He had an aquiline nose and deep-set brown-black eyes, edged with thick black lashes. His face was olive-tanned and very kind. His light brown hair was gathered at the back into a pony-tail. He wasn't wearing classic spirit robes but an open-necked white shirt and loose-fitting black jeans.

It was all such a natural scene, I might have been on a country picnic. The children who had gathered around him ranged from the ages of about six to twelve and they were quietly attentive in the coolness, listening to him.

'Now: we're going to use the power of our thoughts to create our surroundings,' he announced.

There was immediate excitement in the group: the youngsters began whispering confidentially amongst themselves. But he didn't stop them; he simply smiled and waited patiently.

'Right, I'm going to build something in the palm of my hand simply by using the power of my mind.'

'How?' asked a Chinese girl who spoke with an American accent.

'How do you think?' he smiled.

A blond English boy who was aged about ten chipped in:

'Well, whenever I made something back home,' he said, 'I used to gather the materials first, before I could put it together.'

'That's right, Andrew, and it's exactly the same here — only the method of gathering is slightly different.'

'Is it by Thought, Guy?'

'Yes, that's exactly right. Everything is a thought, isn't it?'

'Yes,' said Andrew again. And there was general agreement amongst the children, after which their tutor continued:

'By thinking hard and really concentrating our thoughts single-mindedly, we can draw together the necessary substances from the atmosphere and create something. Thought is more powerful here than it is on Earth; it has a more *direct* effect on our ether, on our surroundings.

'But it isn't easy, by any means. It takes a good deal of effort.

'On the mother planet we'd have to physically chop down a tree before we could burn its logs for heat. But even then we couldn't do any of that without first taking thought, could we children?'

'No,' they chorused in staggered sound.

'In this new world we don't gather things physically but spiritually, by using the drawing power of our thoughts. Now — what shall we make?'

'I'd like a pencil,' said the Chinese girl.

'Right.'

'A *red* pencil,' she added.

'OK. Let's see if I can get it for you. I have to think quite hard when I do this: one small thought isn't enough — it has to be a real effort on my part. I must "see" and hold the form of the solid object in my mind before it can be projected outwards and materialise in my hands.'

He then held out his two palms, cupped them together and closed his eyes.

A tangible silence fell over his captive young audience.

He was immersed in deep concentration, which delighted the youngsters no end. They pointed at his features and whispered amongst themselves, as children do; and wondered whether or not he'd be successful and get the colour just right. (Because if it didn't turn out to be red, the Chinese girl told them quite categorically that she didn't want it!)

After a short time, something started 'hazing' or 'misting' in his palms.

The red pencil gradually took shape, became visible and solidified; and soon it was permanently present as a tangible and useful object.

The youngsters laughed and applauded cheerfully as Guy threw the pencil to the delighted young girl.

'Now you must all try it,' he smiled at his charges; and here I mysteriously lost the class...

But between the two worlds, while I journeyed quickly back to Earth, I caught my guide's deep voice announcing:

'Tomorrow night I shall be privileged to accompany you on a visit to a Higher Sphere of Brilliance and Light — and there we shall meet someone very special...'

15

The Shining Ones

I

'Hold fast to my hand, and whatever you do: do not let go,' cautioned White Owl, 'for tonight we shall visit deep into the Realms of Light where the Shining Ones dwell and without my power you cannot travel there.'

At this, the misty surroundings of the astral world began to shiver to my sight. Then our hands touched and I felt a tremendous surge of electrical power — life-energy — transferring itself from him to me; power which quickened up the vibrations of my spirit body and I began to feel nervous.

'Be at ease and enjoy the lightness of soul,' he said.

'I'll try.'

But I was still rather concerned about

what was happening, for now we were surrounded by nothing which was recognisable – just pastel colours, swirling and blending together so beautifully and quickly that they took my breath clean away. It was such a wonderful sight, but so strange — and it was accompanied by indescribable soul sensations that made me feel quite emotional.

Now I felt as light as a feather, electrically 'alive' and so full of awareness because my vibrations had been lifted to such a pitch that every fibre of my spirit body tingled with energy. I felt super-aware, super-conscious, as we seemed to be arriving in some Higher Spheres.

'Do not attempt to speak,' said my guide, 'until you have acclimatised yourself to the finer environment, my friend. And whatever you do – keep hold of my hand.'

I nodded.

A part of me realised that he was my power-link to this sphere and the rest of me was mystified by what had happened.

He instantly 'knew' these concerns, so with his deep and mellow thought-voice he advised:

'None here speak with their mouths; we transfer intentions and ideas by thought. You are to be given a rare glimpse into life in worlds so far removed from Earth that, at first, you may not comprehend all you see. But it is enough to witness and remember. Later, you will understand.'

I then 'heard' my own thought-voice for the first time as clear as a crisp church bell: it sounded its automatic response, which made my teacher laugh aloud (in his mind, of course) — because I'd thought, *'I'll have to behave myself.'*

'You would not be here, if you could not,' was his amusing retort.

'Are we expected?' I thought again.

'Nothing goes unnoticed in these realms; the Power of the Mind is Supreme, as I have always taught you. But here it's potency will amaze even yourself!' he said, smiling like a wise old man; after which his deep eyes indicated I should look ahead. I obeyed as I felt him clasp my hand more tightly and I responded likewise.

All around us was a fine transparent cloud of pink, green and blue pastel-coloured mist wafting gently in the atmosphere. Then suddenly, and quietly, it swirled aside to reveal a scene of beautiful light. Everything in this place, which didn't resemble a room, a house or even countryside, seemed to have been 'crafted', 'sculptured' or, perhaps more correctly, *created* out of light. And within this cloudy self-illuminated world, brilliant points of different coloured light, like twinkling stars, were moving gracefully about in all directions: some fast, some very slow.

Their colours were of every known and unknown hue, glowing with an unearthly iridescence.

Through this all-pervading light I could see no angels playing heavenly lyres (though I confess I wouldn't have been surprised if I had; so magnificent was the scene). No, there was just a soft yet radiantly diffused glow filling my vision, a wondrous fogbank of pastel energies.

Many questions immediately flashed through my mind, all of which became 'real' the moment they were born.

'Be still, and know that I Am God,' said White Owl; and I thought he meant we were in the presence of — or certainly near to — beings whose task it was to guide the worlds of spirit by Thought.

But I was completely wrong.

'We are approaching only the lowlands of the spheres of light wherein dwell beings whose tasks are to tend various seemingly insentient life-forms on Mother Earth. This sector contains elemental spirits serving some of the planet's vegetation and animal life.'

'Are we near any animals?'

'No: you are in the presence of some of the guiding forces of Nature.'

'These beings have no form,' I said, a note of surprise in my thought-voice.

'But they do. You have only just approximated to this sphere and your perceptions are not yet finely attuned. Clear your vision and discover where you are.'

'But I thought we'd arrived somewhere really high in the spirit world.'

'No; that is yet to come. Look again and see!'

So I sharpened my sight and watched in wonderment as the pastel clouds slowly parted and drifted away, leaving only the bright pinpoints of light dancing in the air, in the midst of a lovely rural scene filled with thick vegetation. The colours of the plants were almost shining and even their foliage was 'alive' with a vibrancy that I could acutely sense and feel.

'This is Earth, my friend. These fields of flowers and hedgerows are near the borders of the South of France.'

'But I thought...'

'I've imparted but a fraction of my power to speed up your spirit body to approximate to the rate whereby these nature spirits can be seen.'

'I'm attuned to their frequencies?'

'Yes.'

Excitedly, I looked all around me and saw that within each dancing light (which moved from flowers to branches in all different directions, touching and examining different plants) there was a tiny being at its centre.

'Move forward,' was the gentle suggestion from my guide, when I wondered if I might touch one. 'Stretch out your hand and do not be afraid, for they are easily frightened even though they are sometimes rather mischievous. They avoid creatures whose hearts are impure or whose minds harbour fear or hostile negativity. But they are very amiable little beings, once they have accepted you as a friend.'

Gently, almost without thinking, I slowly extended the open flat palm of my free left hand, rather as one might do when inviting a wild bird to feed on a few grains in it. Soon, there was a little flurry of activity nearby and four or five of the dancing lights approached, gliding on the air.

I marvelled at the opportunity to study them at close quarters, incredulously viewing the tiny life-forms within their radiant egg-sized globes, and noticing that it was the bodies of the forms themselves which radiated these wonderful auras. The electro-magnetic lights were of various swirling hues: golds, blues, pinks, greens, and even some with reddish colours.

Then quite spontaneously, one of the little people alighted on my hand. To my amazement, I peered into its form and discovered what appeared to be a young slim naked woman within the light. Sporting flesh-coloured skin (seemingly made of the light itself, but perhaps containing more pale yellow shades than our skin tones) she was the proud owner of piercing pale blue eyes. Her long silvery hair, fine in texture and almost platinum in colour, was parted in the centre of her head and long enough to fall well below her waist; she kept brushing it gently aside as she studied my features.

This little nature spirit showed no outward signs of gender, no sexual organs or breasts, but just a pleasing young female form which seemed to glow and project such natural grace and gentleness of spirit.

Gazing intently at each other, we were both enchanted by the other's appearance; she was rather coy, while I was completely fascinated.

I noticed she had *four* fingers on each hand and *four* toes on each foot, and attached to the back of her shoulders there was a pair of almost dragonfly-like translucent gossamer wings which quivered and shook with life. The little person chuckled as I moved my large eyes back and forth to examine her vibrant and perfectly formed body, which seemed to have been created out of nothing more than the ethereal light she was bathed in.

While standing on my palm and weighing virtually nothing, she turned that I might see her wings more closely (she was well aware of my interest in them).

Then with another faint chuckle she fluttered them quickly back and forth and suddenly sailed up into the air and over to some nearby flowers.

Like a tiny flock of birds, her friends who'd also come to see me (and they didn't all look the same, some of them were obviously male) instantly followed her and, in a moment, they were flying around the brightly-lit stamens within some blossoms. They were just like busy insects tending to the job of cross-fertilisation; only, from their bodies they seemed to discharge life-energies to the essence of the flowers instead of pollen.

'They are the divas of these plants,' said my teacher.

'Can they speak?'

'Yes, though not in a language you or I understand. But she knew your thoughts and displayed her wings.'

'I've seen drawings of these creatures,' I said.

'Yes; and why do you think their images have been captured so well?'

And I instinctively knew what he meant: that in everything which may seem to have been created by vivid imagination, grains of truth might well reside.

Immediately after these ideas occurred, I lost touch with my visions and can't recall the next steps in our journey...

II

...But consciousness fades back as both my guide and I were standing at the foot of some impressive mountains. Their mighty peaks were high and majestic, purple-headed and stunningly beautiful. They seemed to almost touch the sky and were ranged for so many miles around us that I couldn't properly distinguish an horizon at all.

'There is to be a visit,' he smiled. 'Someone

who commands great respect in these lands is coming soon.'

'But I thought there was no government here,' I replied.

'And there isn't – not as you know it on Earth. But we do have hierarchies, respected individuals and groups of ancient souls who are renowned for their great wisdom, knowledge and experience which they have attained through many existences.'

'How long have they existed?'

'Countless centuries, aeons. There are many souls here upon whom it would be difficult, if not impossible, to place an exact age. Timeless in Essence, they administer their wise judgement to any in need of it. And one of the most advanced souls in this plane has informed us of the impending arrival of such a Shining One.'

'Us?'

'The Group of Souls whom I count as my Brothers and Sisters, though not in terms of blood but soul-affinity.'

'Who is coming?' I asked.

'You will see. In fact, I do not think she will be alone; there may well be a group visitation.'

'Why?' I asked, within my mind. 'Why have I been permitted this honour when I obviously haven't earned it? I have no right to share in such a wonderful occasion.'

'But you have,' he said. 'No one here is allowed an experience unless they need it.'

'I've earned the right?'

'Of course you have. You presently cannot remember, but it is no mistake that you are here. Did you think I simply decided to bring you?'

I wanted to naively answer 'yes', but I felt ashamed of my lack of understanding; a feeling which made him smile.

After an amused silence, during which both he and I took great delight in drawing upon the life-giving rarefied air and marvelling at the wonderful purple-headed peaks, he resumed:

'You could not be here in these spheres without my power; and I could not have given it to you without the permission of greater minds who guide these heavens. If your presence here would be imprudent then it would have been prevented. But, fortunately, they see much further forward into our existences than we can presently imagine.'

He turned his face away from the mountains and looked directly into my eyes. 'There are reasons why,' he said, 'and I daresay these will eventually become clear to us both.'

'How would you have been prevented from bringing me?'

'My power would have been withdrawn; and so would you.'

'Would I have been harmed?'

'No, just quietly removed. You would have woken back within the confines of your physical body and your memory of the effort would have been completely buried, "forgotten".'

'But I understood these kingdoms weren't controlled by governments like we have on Earth. Politics and temporal rulers are often so corrupt.'

'True, but not here. In these realms the Great Spirit rules Supreme. God is the only Governor, whose Laws are Just and Wholesome and certainly not corrupt.

'Here each sphere has many progressed minds existing within it who, because of their great experience, have naturally earned access to knowledge about which we can at present only dream. So vast are the parameters of these spiritual worlds, God has ordained it that everywhere one travels there will always be advanced minds monitoring our thoughts and actions.

'In these realms we cannot escape being fully known and understood; no more than

335

you on Earth can avoid our attention —
should we desire to give it.'

I shivered at the thought of all our actions
being registered, but realised that only
when this fact truly dawns in our minds
would humanity undertake, in real earnest,
the long process of continually purifying its
thoughts. I was then compelled to ask:

'Do we have any privacy on Earth?'

'Of a kind,' he smiled. 'For the most part a
person's Earth-life trundles by in ordained
paths without us viewing each act and deed.
But there is no one with you who can
prevent us monitoring certain events, if we
consider it beneficial to do so.'

'But who permits it?' I asked.

'The Great Spirit, who has ordained us
with the Power to see.'

Then his speech fell away, for there came
a perceptible change in the atmosphere — it
shivered, as if an earthquake were about to
occur. I quickly discerned this to be the
announcement of an imminent arrival
further up at the top of the mountains.

'Quite correctly perceived,' he said, 'and we
must go to the plateau where our friends
are waiting. We are to witness the arrival
Sheerah and her attendants.'

'Sheerah?'

'One of the most progressed spirits and

evolved minds connected with this sphere; indeed an old and wise soul.'

'A Shining One?'

'Yes. Come! We must not keep our welcoming party waiting.'

I knew we would then make the instant journey to the top of the mountains. I was right. Within a microsecond — no, sooner — we were right in the midst of a group of about twenty Enlightened Ones who projected such sincere soul-warmth that I immediately felt at ease.

Then something odd happened: as soon as our presence was felt, White Owl released my hand. A little surge of panic made me clumsily reach out to take his arm again but he withdrew it. Suddenly I realised that I was safe within the centre of this circle of advanced souls, who had gathered silently around a nook near to a rocky cave entrance. In the same instant I also knew that their collected power was supporting my vibrations and I no longer needed my guide's help.

All at once, almost in unison, every head turned in my direction and the finely featured human beings (robed in light of differing hues) smiled and strangely nodded in greeting. I was pleased, but slightly embarrassed. I returned the compliment by slightly inclining my head. As I did so, I was aware of having met or known each of these people, but I couldn't quite remember when or where.

White Owl stepped to my side and the entire mountain atmosphere altered again, almost impelling us to face a raised rocky nook nearby. We duly obeyed and then watched enthralled as a brilliant golden mist gradually appeared from thin air and gently condensed, until within it we could just about perceive the forms of four people, one standing far forward of the other three.

As the hazy shapes materialised and solidified, there was revealed to us a beautiful woman with golden hair — an Angel of Light. She was wearing a lilac-coloured robe which seemed to be a part of herself. Her eyes were deep blue-green like unfathomed ocean waters. Her remarkably penetrating gaze conveyed to me the most wonderful sense of peace that I've ever experienced in the spirit spheres.

She was serenity personified; a delicate but powerful angel, without wings.

Slowly, she looked around the gathering and nodded to her companions in the crowd, who each touched their heads, or bowed and reverently acknowledged her presence.

Her three attendants in the background

were all male, each wearing a long robe: one wore pale green, one pale blue and another was clad in a similar shade to Sheerah's attire. The men were all over six feet in height, but Sheerah was only about five feet tall. Yet she radiated the purest light and the most powerful aura of us all. I required no effort to sense her greatness of heart, her clarity of thought and the deep and powerful well of Love she carried in her soul for every thing in Creation – these qualities were almost tangible.

No one uttered a syllable as her expansive mind stretched out and touched us, enfolding us within her power until we almost felt we were an integral part of her great self.

She was undoubtedly a very advanced soul of great age and wisdom, but concealed beneath shapely youth and radiant beauty.

After she'd greeted her friends and given each one of them a personal message of encouragement for the work which had been done near to Earth in the name of love and peace, her compassionate gaze turned upon me and her thoughts touched me:

'There are no mistakes. You have been summoned, for there is much work for you to do.'

'If I can do it, I will,' I replied.

A murmur of approval moved within the minds of the assembly.

'The kingdom of Earth is for ever a place of toil and woe. Part of its function in the Divine Plan is to provide searing blows to the spirit which will help it to grow. But the human race needs Light.'

'I agree,' I said.

'The Planet is daily being abused and systematically ruined. Its forests are being destroyed. These are the Mother's great lungs which produce life-giving oxygen. Without them the atmosphere will deteriorate and life is threatened.'

'I know,' I said.

'Ask man to care. Instruct him to plant new trees, purify the air and do everything in his power to keep the Mother's pulse beating for centuries to come. Global warming spells disaster for the Children of the Earth, but still not enough minds take immediate action.'

'Isn't it all part of a plan?' I asked.

'Yes,' she returned kindly, 'as indeed is this request, lovingly given to those who follow you.'

Put gently in my place, I apologised for my hasty remark and asked what else I might do to help.

'Instruct Man to think forward: his actions

today affect his Mother tomorrow. The pollution which poisons her veins is speeding up at an alarming rate. Her once-pure streams and soils are now thickly clogged with harmful chemicals.'

'What of her people?' I asked.

'Tend to them lovingly, but I am charged to speak of the Planet.'

'What can I do?'

'Tell all those who will listen to care for her. Record our meeting and people will be touched as these warnings are given.'

'But I forget so much when I wake.'

'You will be helped by these powers,' she said, indicating with a graceful arm the small gathering of teachers all around me. 'You will not forget me, or my thoughts. I shall attend to it.'

And with this, a ray of silver light shot out from the centre of her forehead and touched the centre of mine. As it struck, I felt overwhelmed by a great peacefulness and also knew that certain information had been 'branded' on my mind; that's the only way I can describe it.

'You will not recall our meeting until the time is right,' she went on, 'only then will this memory surface, and you will write.'

'Yes,' I said. 'I'll do whatever I can.

Another soul present asked:

'Sheerah, what will be the outcome?'

'I regret,' she replied gracefully, 'I am not yet permitted to reveal this, my friend.'

The teacher acknowledged her decision and respected her reply.

She then upheld her right arm and hand and from it a soft but radiant bluish-gold light spurted upwards like a fountain of stars, cascading over all the gathering who straightened their backs under its caress. Then she spoke again to the group.

'Peace be with you. The work of spiritualising Man is progressing as it was meant to do. Never tire of your duties, my dear friends; and encourage your charges to serve the race with loving compassion, for the work is never over.'

That was when I realised that these teachers were all spirit guides: each one was connected with a separate medium, or mediums, on Earth.

A quiet respect fell about the group.

'The Shining Ones, higher in status and wisdom than any of ourselves, send you their Blessing.'

Expectancy filled the air...

'The Masters of Light are pleased with what has been achieved thus far; even though our brothers and sisters in the flesh are, for the most part, still spiritually asleep, much has been accomplished.

'The Wise Ones will never cease from pouring out their guidance to touch and inspire you in the various spheres of your activity. Personal instructions will soon be transmitted to each one of you.'

Then her wise counsel revealed just who the spiritual teachers gathered in that silent place truly were:

'Keep the souls of those nations in your charge firmly thinking along the lines of harmony between all facets of the Great Spirit's Creation.

'Renounce all doubts and be glad: the work is moving forward; and we, with the Invincible Power of Love, are winning the battle over materialism, greed and cruelty.

'The Love of the Masters is with you, now and always.

'The Shining Ones will guide each one.

'You have only but to call upon their names to seek their Inspiration and their unceasing Blessing.'

And an audible sigh travelled through the assembly.

They were truly thankful.

They were refreshed and renewed.

They felt greater peace for having touched this Shining Soul's presence. They were grateful for receiving again her continued commitment to aid them with their spiritual work.

The perfect stillness came to an end when the silence was broken by Sheerah's final thought:

'Peace...' she said, as the whole scene dissolved away before my gaze...

Epilogue

It formed itself and came to me in a dream, the kind of lucid picture-book experience that's full of moving kaleidoscopic images which remain long after waking.

Quietly, I yawned, rose, stretched and set about making the vision a reality.

I opened the moisture-proof box and carefully placed each item inside: first a poster, then a colour picture-programme, followed by a copy of my birth certificate, some inspirational poetry cards and a photograph of a pastel portrait of me and my spirit friend, White Owl. I added one of the audio-tapes I'd recorded, plus a letter and other bits and pieces.

On top of all this I laid three of my books: *Visions Of Another World*, *Voices From Heaven* and the manuscript of *In Touch With Eternity*; a trilogy of psychic and spiritual adventures interwoven with spirit teachings, for discerning eyes to view.

I closed the box.

After completely sealing it, I loaded the precious booty into the car and drove alone through country fields. I eventually stopped and walked into a misty afternoon that was kissing rolling fields, somewhere deep in the heart of Wales, the nation of my birth.

Unseen, I carried the time-capsule far out into a peaceful green place where I thought it would never be discovered by the hands or machines of modern-day man. As a final precaution I scanned the horizon, seeking any sign of human life.

There was none.

I was physically alone.

I took the spade and dug a hole about three feet deep and then knelt beside it on soft Welsh soil. I closed my eyes against the sun and spoke a few words of thankfulness to the Spirit People, without whom very few of the thousands of words I've written would have had any real meaning, for they had inspired me very step of the way.

'Thank you for your teachings, guidance and love. I gave you my promise that I would serve; and I've kept it. I've shared the truth with others,' I said.

Then I opened my eyes to nothing but silence all around, though I did sense invisible presences close by... watching, listening, thinking.

In fact, it was they who had indicated the exact spot where this time-capsule should be entombed; this small piece of Yesterday, buried Today, to be found by someone of a distant Tomorrow.

'I'll never reveal its location,' I affirmed softly, heard only by a flock of singing birds.

The long drive home gave me plenty of time for reflection. Just like watching an old-time flickering movie, I remembered dozens of different scenes: my pathway; the years of gruelling work and nationwide touring; the perspiration and struggle; and the secret healing and spiritual guidance I'd so gladly received when all Earthly souls had deserted me.

Despite a sweeping melancholy, I was very grateful, for it occurred to me that perhaps in centuries to come — in the next millennia — the capsule might suddenly be unearthed and its contents may be studied by men of another time...

*

That night, lying in my warm bed, I pondered on the reaction of some future archaeologist as his fingers smoothed the sealed container.

I was fascinated.

Perhaps, in this remote future, our present form of English would no longer be used or by then it might be unrecognisable? Our discoverer would have to painstakingly piece together fragmented writings and carefully translate them as best he could — like his ancestors did after finding the Dead Sea Scrolls.

I turned out the bedside lamp and tucked myself further under the warm sheets.

In the darkness I could almost see his puzzled expression as a million questions galloped through the fields of his mind. Would he wonder what in heaven he'd unearthed?

Who was this man? Was he a teacher? A reformer? A challenger of thoughts?

Could he have been a messenger who spoke with angels?

Was he some kind of healer, a worker of wonders?

And if he was a man of God, where are the rest of his teachings hidden?

Under the duvet I wrapped my tired limbs in these distant thoughts and smiled, thinking, 'Perhaps I'm all those of things, possibly some; in certain eyes, maybe none.'

(Though I've loved the soul of man, its

expression through personality has frequently left much to be desired.)

Half-asleep, I continued musing.

'There's plenty more to achieve. I haven't written about spiritual unfoldment or mediumistic development yet, or recorded my philosophy on the conduct of the soul; not fully, anyway. Then there's my poetry: yes, I've plenty more to share — if it's part of my Life-Plan.'

Wispy dreams threaded through the chasms of my mind; and I must have closed my eyes and started to gently drift into peaceful reverie.

The faraway downstairs clock chimed out the hollow hour. It was now past midnight; tomorrow already... and the rain was pelting against the bedroom windows.

But before unconsciousness fully embraced me, I remembered that in the coming evening — tonight, at 7.30 — I'd be standing again upon another stage, in another city, facing another thousand strangers desperately wanting news of their loved-ones in the next world.

They will have queued in the downpour and then filled rows of seats with a sea of hopeful faces... eyes twinkling in the lights and brimming with expectancy.

They'll want me to succeed.

And no matter how easy or difficult my work may be, through it all they'll expect me to smile, even if my spirit is wracked with sorrow and my heart is breaking in two.

But then, I mustn't allow myself the luxury of complaining. A servant of the Spirit must deny this right, he must hide his own feelings – and serve.

Inside this darkness, the spotlight will pick me out and carry me through the meeting, high on a wave of love generated by the people.

Distant thunder cracked these images then rolled like giant empty oil-drums around the skies; and the room lit up with sheets of lightning.

I curled up into a snug ball, pulled the bedclothes high up, further over my head, and wrapped myself in the velvet night, half whispering as I fell asleep:

'Don't worry, I'll be there... and I'll do my best.

'God willing, I won't let you down...'

* * *

For further information on all aspects of the
life and work of visionary, spiritual healer,
medium and poet, Stephen O'Brien,
including how to obtain by Mail Order
his best-selling books, educational cassettes,
spiritual healing crystals, and a full range of
other quality products (or to contact him directly)
please write, enclosing a large SAE, to:

VOICES MANAGEMENT
(Dept VB3)
PO Box 8
SWANSEA
SA1 1BL
UK

Or search the Internet for 'Stephen O'Brien'.

Voices Management regrets it cannot reply
without a large stamped self-addressed envelope
and correspondents are respectfully advised
not to mail irreplaceable items to the author,
for neither Voices, nor Mr O'Brien,
can accept responsibility for the loss or damage
of any unsolicited manuscripts, poems,
sentimental objects, photographs, or cassettes, etc.,
which are often posted by the public.

Your letters are always welcome,
but please keep them brief and to the point —
and be patient when awaiting your replies,
for Stephen receives vast quantities of mail
from around the world.

Thank you.

ANGELS BY MY SIDE
BY STEPHEN O'BRIEN:

Stephen O'Brien's extraordinary spiritual and psychic gifts have comforted millions of people and have silenced sceptics around the world. Stephen reveals through his acclaimed powers: What kind of life awaits us all after death, and the secrets of the Next World; Impressive evidence of survival; The secret Psychic Powers of Light and Colour that enhance well-being and self-healing; A compelling view of 'The One Living God'. Through more of his amazing Out-of-the-Body excursions into the Spirit World itself, he also shares with his countless readers: Timeless Wisdom from the 'Silent Sentinels' and Angel Beings who watch over us, and he unveils fascinating glimpses into mankind's future.

A Voices Paperback (384 pages; illustrated)
ISBN: 0-9536620-0-4

A GIFT OF GOLDEN LIGHT
BY STEPHEN O'BRIEN:

Follow Stephen as he recalls his exciting 20-year psychic apprenticeship and strives to perfect the extraordinary paranormal skills which have brought happiness, comfort and hope to millions of people. With warmth and candour, he shares his thrilling encounters with apparitions, hauntings, spiritual healing and telepathic powers; presents a compelling array of survival evidence of human and animal souls after death; and reveals the mystical Gift of Golden Light which illuminates everyone's spiritual journey through life.

The Press described this book as 'un-put-downable'.

A Voices Paperback (384 pages; illustrated)
ISBN: 0-9536620-1-2

'The epitome of mediumistic excellence' – *Psychic News*

Available from our worldwide mail order service, or order them through all good book stores and libraries.